BIG CON
AUSTRALIA'S UNKNOWN SOCCER PIONEER

BIG CON
AUSTRALIA'S UNKNOWN SOCCER PIONEER

TREVOR THOMPSON

FAIRPLAY
PUBLISHING

First published in 2025 by Fair Play Publishing

PO Box 4101, Balgowlah Heights, NSW 2093, Australia
www.fairplaypublishing.com.au

ISBN: 978-1-923236-31-8
ISBN: 978-1-923236-32-5 (ePub)

© Trevor Thompson 2025

The moral rights of the author have been asserted.
All rights reserved. Except as permitted under the *Australian Copyright Act 1968*
(for example, a fair dealing for the purposes of study, research, criticism or review),
no part of this book may be reproduced, stored in a retrieval system,
communicated or transmitted in any form or by any means without prior
written permission from the Publisher.

Design and typesetting by Leslie Priestley.
Front cover photograph of Con Jones from the British Columbia Soccer Hall of Fame.
Back cover photograph of Con Jones's personal scrapbook
by Trevor Thompson via the John Fuller Collection.

All inquiries should be made to the Publisher via hello@fairplaypublishing.com.au

A catalogue record of this book is available from the National Library of Australia.

Contents

Introduction		1
Chapter 1	The Death of Thomas Shortel	4
Chapter 2	1904 – The Future Is Here	8
Chapter 3	The Shortels	13
Chapter 4	The Süssmilchs	19
Chapter 5	Pacific Soccer League	23
Chapter 6	George Arthur Parker – King of Empire Football	26
Chapter 7	The People Shield	29
Chapter 8	Don't Argue – Con Jones in Vancouver	32
Chapter 9	Con Jones, Lacrosse and More	36
Chapter 10	Con Jones the Pirate and his Swashbuckling Mates	40
Chapter 11	Will Ellis – Vancouver's New Zealander	46
Chapter 12	Global Football	48
Chapter 13	Australia's North American Tour	52
Chapter 14	Trans-Pacific Australians	56
Chapter 15	Con Jones in Britain	60
Chapter 16	Con Jones Stadium - Vancouver Soccer's Spiritual Home	64

Chapter 17	Canada and the South Pacific	68
Chapter 18	The Scandalous Daughter	72
Chapter 19	The Con Jones Method	77
Chapter 20	Remembering Con Jones	80
	End Notes	88
	Acknowledgements	89

Introduction

Con Jones was a Sydney-born soccer pioneer who remains unknown in his home country. Even the most dedicated fans have never heard of his remarkable rise from orphaned street kid and adolescent prisoner to sports promoter negotiating with international football's top decision-makers.

He left Australia in 1903 at the age of 34 with no experience in the game, but he became its most significant promoter in his adopted home of Vancouver and a major influence in the soccer culture of Canada. He died after collapsing at a match being played in the stadium he built. He was 59.

His career as a promoter included many sports but his experience in football coincided with the game's rolling thunder of continual expansion and change. His soccer life began in 1904, the year of FIFA's founding, Canada's gold medal at the St. Louis Olympics, and Australia's first international soccer experience in New Zealand.

He died in 1929 on the brink of the first World Cup in Uruguay. The explosion of activity all over the world led to international competitions between clubs and countries in Europe, Latin America and Asia, the emergence of professionalism, the celebration and erosion of English football authority in the world, and the development of the new commercial business of international tours.

Con Jones was the first Australian entrepreneur to engage with this new world.

Jones introduced professional soccer to British Columbia, managed home-and-away tours by teams from British Columbia and California, started a new competition for clubs from both sides of the border, devised a plan for the selection of a national team which was well ahead of its time, and pursued greater contact with touring teams from Britain in talks with the leaders of the Football Association. This included negotiating with the F.A in London as a designated representative of the Dominion of Canada Football Association.

His work linked him to Football Association secretary Frederick Wall, United States soccer kingpin Thomas Cahill and international soccer businessman George Parker, manager of the world's first intercontinental tours, those of the Corinthians club.

Con Jones was never known in any capacity in Australia. In his home city of Sydney, he was Thomas Shortel, a well-known bookie and bookseller who won public approval for his support of the city's poor children by giving them employment selling newspapers on the street. He was also a supporter of charities and the city's cultural life along with his second wife's highly respected German family, the Süssmilchs, who were prominent in music and science.

But Jones was also a thief and a scoundrel whose Australian life came to a scandalous end. As a bookie, he stole thousands of pounds of punters' bets on the 1903 Melbourne Cup and fled to Canada under a new name to escape a warrant for his arrest.

Jones stayed in contact with Australian sport but although family and friends shuttled between Vancouver and Sydney to maintain contact, he stayed beyond the reach of the law and never returned to Australia.

This book examines Jones' work in the broader context of sports promotion in the 20th century era and the rapidly changing nature of the soccer world.

He was the son of an immigrant who became a migrant himself. His personal life was complicated. He was a street kid who went to jail as a 14-year-old. Alcoholism killed his Irish father and eventually two of his own sons. He was the father of seven children by three different women, with custody of one daughter the focus of a dramatic court case. Another daughter went to prison in Queensland after defrauding a string of friends and suitors.

His Canadian business prominence was built on tobacco and gambling ventures. His profile was enhanced by his use of a 'Don't Argue' slogan and logo that were stolen from Australian commerce.

In Canada, he demonstrated business skills that Australia's soccer community sorely lacked. He financed the game in British Columbia at a time when any hint of professionalism was still frowned on by the Sydney establishment, and amateurism was still influential in Vancouver.

While researching his story, I nominated Con Jones for inclusion in the British Columbia Soccer Hall of Fame. He was inducted in late 2023.

Jones was a remarkable trailblazer in soccer history. He is now officially recognised in Canada. He deserves to be recognised in Australia too.

CHAPTER 1
The Death of Thomas Shortel

On a bright sunny Victorian afternoon, over 95,000 people crammed into Flemington racecourse for the running of the Melbourne Cup, an event already referred to by the phrase which became a journalistic cliché, 'the race that stops a nation'. The attendance amounted to about a fifth of the city's population, while masses of punters betting mountains of wagers waited around the country for news of the result.

Sydney bookmaker Tommy Shortel was among those anxiously wondering how the race would transform his fortunes. The sporting theatre of the race would turn out to be no match for the drama about to overwhelm his life.

The day ended with a riot at Shortel's city business premises when an angry mob trashed his offices and threatened the life of his brother-in-law.

The two-mile race had been run on the first Tuesday in November since 1861 and was easily the nation's biggest sporting event. In the lead-up to the 1903 race, press speculation tipped at least half a dozen starters as good chances in an evenly balanced field.

Things changed as race day neared. The well-fancied Hauturier pulled up lame after a training gallop on the weekend before the race and was scratched. Stablemate Emir was also withdrawn. The pre-race elimination of two leading contenders left Abundance and the three-year-old colt Lord Cardigan generally listed as joint favourites at either 5/1 or 6/1.

Both ran well and were favourably placed approaching the home straight. Abundance's jockey said in a post-race interview that he knew his charge had run out of steam and had no more to give in a sprint for the line. Abundance faded to ninth place. St Ambrose led the field at the final turn but 20/1 chance

Wakeful then took the lead only to be run down by a spirited Lord Cardigan in the last few strides to win by three-quarters of a length.

Lord Cardigan was carrying only six stone eight pounds (41.7 kilos) in the race compared to the whopping ten stone (63.5 kilos) of runner-up Wakeful or the nine stone four (59 kilos) of Abundance. Over two miles, the weight difference surely made a difference.

Even so, it had been a skilful ride which catapulted 16-year-old winning jockey Norman Godby to prominence. He went on to be regarded as one of the finest jockeys of his era.

In Sydney, Tom Shortel had been offering a starting price a point higher than most at his bookmaking business next to his newsagency in busy Market Street. The slightly longer odds attracted plenty of money looking for a bigger return.

The victory of a strongly supported favourite meant a liability so big for Tom Shortel that there was no way he could pay out those holding a winning ticket. It may be the case that he never had any intention of paying out and saw the race as a chance to defraud his customers by making off with thousands of pounds for his own use. This would be the fund to finance the project of reinventing his life.

Punters with winning tickets turned up at Shortel's Market Street laneway entrance that evening to find the doors closed, even though the designated seven o'clock settlement time had been reached. They did see that there was a man inside the brightly lit room who they presumed was readying for the payout. The door was opened and a crowd of about 150 crammed in.

According to the *Sydney Sportsman*, the clerk answered a phone call away from the main room and then came back to announce, 'Mr Shortel will settle on Friday next.' The *Sportsman* reported that the clerk did not seem to realise the significance of his announcement, nor that the postponement of payments was seen by the punters as nothing short of a provocation.

The crowd began shouting 'robbery', 'thieves' and 'police' along with rougher language referred to delicately in the paper as 'more forcible adjectives'. The clerk was attacked and had his coat pulled off before he escaped and fled to the fourth floor. He opened the pair of folding doors over a space once used to haul goods in and out of the building and stepped out onto the foot-wide ledge.

He was able to close the doors behind him and remained standing on the ledge, 60 feet (18 metres) above the lane. He simply hoped the police would get to him ahead of the furious punters. Inside, the mob ransacked the offices, wrecked fittings, tore up all paper and books, and threw the letterpress into the lane. Eventually, the police arrived. They could not placate the angry throng, but they did at least rescue the clerk from his two-hour ordeal on the ledge.

Some of the mob went to Shortel's home to demand payment but found only the bookie's heavily pregnant wife and three children. They then went to Central Station to see if he was fleeing town on a late train. Again, no luck.

Back at Shortel's offices, the writing was literally on the wall. Rioting ticket holders had scrawled their vengeful messages wherever they could. 'Gone but not forgotten' was chalked on the blackboard along with the ominous '500 reward for Tommy Shortel, dead or alive. Dead preferred.'

Tommy Shortel was, in effect, already dead. The bookie would never use the name again. He was now Con Jones.

The punters' search efforts at Sydney's Central Station were too late. Shortel was already travelling on the 24-hour trip north to Brisbane. There he boarded a ship bound for Vancouver via Honolulu and Los Angeles under his newly assumed name. He never returned to Australia.

In the days following the city uproar, a warrant for his arrest issued by New South Wales police described him as '5 feet 8 inches high, stout build, fair complexion, fair hair and moustache, full round face, dressed in a light sack suit and Panama hat, and wears gold rimmed spectacles, very talkative'.

His brother Sydney Shortel was also a wanted man – '24 years of age, 5 feet 8 inches high, thin build, dark complexion, no hair on face, dressed in a dark sack suit and straw hat. Arrest desirable. May go to Melbourne or South Africa.'

It is not clear whether the note about Melbourne and South Africa was based on intelligence gathered or whether it was simply a red herring dragged across the trail by friends and family. Sydney Shortel also went to Canada to be Sydney Jones.

The warrants were not issued over the betting scandal but rather an alleged theft of ten pounds from a man named Peter Herbert. Mr Herbert was the Governor of Darlinghurst Gaol at the time of Thomas Shortel's brief incarceration. Nevertheless, the warrant for theft would serve the purpose of holding the men and give police a chance to investigate the scandalous Melbourne Cup betting shakedown. In any case, the warrants proved useless. The men were already well on the way to Canada.

Necessity became the mother of invention. 'Con Jones' would be a man with no history, chequered or otherwise.

He aimed to be the maker of his own destiny, unhindered by the shadows of the past.

CHAPTER 2
1904 – The Future is Here

'Is it true Tom Shortel has gone away for a rest?'
'No, he has gone to AVOID arrest'

This gag appeared in the pages of Sydney's *Truth* just as the newly minted Paula Jones and her children arrived in Vancouver in April 1904.

When Thomas Shortel – Con Jones – made his hasty departure from Sydney in November 1903, his wife Pauline was almost eight months pregnant. She gave birth to Noel, their fourth son, on Boxing Day. Paula, her four sons, and her stepdaughter from Con's first marriage Minnie – now called Amy – arrived in the New Year. The transformation of the reinvented family was under way.

The year of 1904 was also a time of beginnings and births for football. Seven nations signed a declaration in Paris to create the *Federation Internationale de Football Associations*, FIFA, which would go on to be the biggest single sport organisation in the world.

This year saw the first international matches for Australians on a tour of New Zealand by New South Wales, Jones' home state. His adopted country Canada won the football gold medal at the St. Louis Olympics.

All the FIFA founding members were European. Their desire to have an organisation to aid the advancement of international football, especially between national teams, was clear and uncomplicated.

Politically, the move was a step away from the authority of the Football Association in London and its supremacy in all football matters. FIFA embraced the vibrant new reality of international contact and aimed to give the countries of the rapidly expanding football world a greater role in guiding that growth. The F.A. was reluctant to endorse the new organisation and guarded its position as the ultimate authority. Australia and Canada were firmly in the English camp.

In Europe, football countries were already familiar with each other and could generally rely on good transport connections to arrange cross-border matches. National cup and league competitions demonstrated which teams and players were in the top echelon. Selecting representative sides was not a significant problem.

In geographically bigger countries like Australia, Canada, India, China and the United States, the creation of national teams and how they might operate was far from straightforward.

At the 1904 Olympics, Canada won the football gold medal through the Galt F.C. team which had been delegated to represent Canada. They beat two local sides from St. Louis, the only other participants. Football was effectively an exhibition event mostly ignored in a chaotic Olympiad often swamped by the sprawling agenda of the St. Louis World's Fair. Olympic sporting contests began on the first of July but football, the last sport to be completed, had to wait until November to reach its conclusion.

The football event was a small, ramshackle affair but included players in the Canadian squad who enjoyed good careers. Sandy Hall's hat trick against Christian Brothers College in a 7–0 win made him the tournament's joint top scorer. Hall had experience in Scotland before moving to Toronto and after the Olympics he joined English champions Newcastle United. He later scored a hatful of goals in a three-year spell back in Scotland at Dunfermline Athletic.

The new international realm took shape in Australia in 1904, 20 years after the first rejection from London for on-field Anglo-Australian contact. The New South Wales team sailed across the Tasman Sea to tour New Zealand in the first international matches for either country.

A return tour to Australia by New Zealand took place in 1905. The two teams created a tradition without which the modern world game would be unrecognisable. Both sides played in numbered shirts and were the first international teams to do so. Their achievement is still largely ignored in football's first world.

Australia did not yet have a national association. This was a team from NSW because no other state had the resources to take part.

Chile, Uruguay and Argentina started the first South American championship in 1910. Asia's first Far Eastern Games football competition was held in the Philippines in 1913. For the United States and British Empire countries, international football dreamers looked to European homelands to offer a chance. The new international commerce of football team tours was to be the means of establishing links between the Old and the New Worlds.

Jones arrived in Los Angeles *en route* to his new home. His disembarkation form shows he told officials he was heading for St. Louis. Whether this was to throw pursuers off his trail, see friends, find out about the yet to begin World's Fair, or whether there was already a pre-arranged sporting purpose in such a trip is hard to tell.

St. Louis was already an important centre for American soccer and the main city in the west of the United States developing a strong soccer culture. Two men dominated this scene, and both influenced Con Jones. They were Winton E. Barker and Thomas W. Cahill.

Barker was the president of the lively St. Louis university campus league starting to attract attention from the eastern states, while Cahill had been managing local sides St. Louis Spaldings and Diel F.C. Cahill had already begun to report on the vibrant soccer scene in the local press. His later journalism at the *Spalding's Official Association Soccer Foot Ball Guide* provided a crucial record of domestic and international football as seen from the United States. Both men were ambitious, capable and eager to push ideas for a bigger profile and nationwide projects for the soccer cause.

Both men were also avowed internationalists.

In 1905, an English team toured the U.S. and Canada for the first time. A middling collection of amateur players known as the Pilgrims and led by the well-credentialled captain Fred Milnes won 14 of 17 matches.

The team's intriguing entourage included John Bentley, a founding member and one-time president of the Football League. He also had a spell as editor of the *Athletic News* and later became vice president of the Football Association. Another guest was Baron William von Reiffenstein, a friend and associate of Baron Pierre de Coubertin at the time of the Frenchman's efforts in the early 1890s to establish the inaugural modern Olympic Games in 1896.

Barker financed the 1905 tour, Cahill managed it.

The higher-profile Corinthians had visited in 1906 but their subsequent tour in 1911 was the first to reach the Pacific coast with four of their 16 Canadian fixtures taking place in British Columbia. By this time, Jones was an influential figure in B.C. sport, and an increasingly important soccer promoter who had acquired a national profile in soccer and lacrosse.

The 1906 tour introduced Jones to G.A.(George) Parker, the most prominent international soccer promoter in the British Empire. Parker was connected to the highest levels of football administration in England and had arranged and managed two Corinthians tours of South Africa.

Parker had not only managed the tours of the most famous amateur team in the world; he also made them into profitable commercial operations. They were so successful that questions were raised about whether Corinthians could continue to be regarded as the paragons of amateur virtue that their image proclaimed them to be.

Parker would soon deliver the People Shield competition into the hands of Con Jones.

By 1906, Jones had established a profile in sport and recreation as the new manager of Vancouver's English Bay Bathing and Athletics Club. The club rooms struck an imposing presence overlooking the beach at scenic English Bay. The club building was impressive, but the club's financial situation was deteriorating. Within a couple of years, the name disappeared. The club was swept up by Jones and became the National Club, operating from premises in east Vancouver. The National Club proved to be a very useful base for a range of Jones' initiatives.

As a sports businessman, Jones was obviously interested in making a dollar. He wasn't above presenting novelty sports events with humour derived from the ethnic backgrounds of the players.

A festive Dominion Day carnival staged to raise money for Vancouver Hospital yielded 1,000 dollars. A tug-o-war contest featuring Chinese, Japanese and Hindu teams preceded what was described as 'the most novel and laughable attraction ever seen in Vancouver,' which was 'a side-splitting football match between the Hindus, Indians, Japanese and Chinese.' This was his first soccer promotion.

The event was so successful that Jones was reported to be taking the event on the road as a travelling show.

Competitions aspiring to be regarded as Canada's national championship for club soccer came and went without ever really establishing a solidly credible claim. *The People* Shield, usually referred to as the People's Shield, was one of them, brought to Canada by Parker as a representative of London's People newspaper, and temporarily passed into the hands of Jones.

The People underwrote the 1906 Corinthians tour and Parker presented the trophy he brought across the Atlantic as a prize to be awarded to Canada's champion team. The subsequent competition for the trophy had a patchy record in attracting support, but for Jones it at least proved to be a useful tool in raising his profile beyond British Columbia.

The Shield gave Jones a platform for one of his big soccer ideas that directly addressed the question of how to select a national team.

The Con Jones-Will Ellis plan promoted the meritocratic notion that a national team should be comprised of the best players available based on performances at the highest level the country could offer rather than one chosen by a committee considering regional recommendations. It had participation in the world's premier international competition as it objective.

These two principles are accepted without question in modern football but were innovations for their times. The formula was well ahead of the systems which came into force in other big countries whose football centres were located far away from each other. For example, China staged an inter-regional tournament which gave the winner the right to represent China.

When Australia finally played full international matches on a tour of New Zealand in 1922, the side only drew on players from the two states prepared to financially back the venture – New South Wales and Queensland. The idea that a national team had to feature players from each of its constituent states governed Australia for decades and shaped the squad picked for Australia's first ever tournament, the 1956 Melbourne Olympics.

However, the Jones-Ellis proposal in the first decade of the 20the century came to nothing as the financially strapped Canadian Olympic Games Committee opted to only support teams or individuals it believed had a genuine chance to win medals at the 1908 London Olympics. The country's footballers were believed to be short of the level required to stand a chance of reaching the podium despite their gold-medal performance in St Louis in 1904.

This may have been so, but it was a colonialist presumption that was never tested. The touring Canadians of 1888 had been dismissed in this way too, but their record in Britain showed them to be far better than their critics predicted.

A Canadian voice directing the course of the team may well have proven to be more valuable than the internalised values of the Old World. Football's New World countries began to spawn fresh ideas to deal with their own circumstances. Con Jones was one of the new players.

CHAPTER 3
The Shortels

At the turn of the century, Thomas Shortel had risen to a position of respect in colonial Sydney. He ran a newspaper and bookselling business in the heart of the city at the turn of the 20th century., although horse race bookmaking was most likely his biggest source of income.

His employment of poor street kids showed a philanthropic side which earned him respect among the great and good of the city, and his marriage connected him with prominent figures in arts and sciences.

He had come a long way from his teenage days of petty crime and incarceration in Darlinghurst Gaol.

Young Thomas was born in Sydney in 1869, the son of Irish parents Thomas Shortel and Theresa Campbell. His father came to Australia via England and New Zealand and worked as a tailor. He became an active unionist, was a member of the Trades Hall Committee, and represented the Tailors Society at the Intercolonial Trades Union Congress in 1885.

Tom Shortel senior arrived in Sydney from New Zealand in 1864 along with his best friend, French-born New Zealand tailor Felix Choisy. The two men married Irish sisters in the same ceremony in 1867. Tom married Theresa Campbell; Felix married Margaret.

The new Shortel family was beset by the deaths of Thomas's siblings. Theresa herself died in 1880 at the age of 31 when her son Thomas was just 11 years old. The stability of the household suffered greatly after her demise.

Thomas senior had regular spells in custody due to drunkenness until his death in Darlinghurst Gaol in 1886. Shortel was admitted to the Receiving House from the Water Police Court and from there went to the gaol hospital where he died two days later.

Dr Maurice O'Connor told an inquest that the deceased had been suffering from nervous exhaustion resulting from delirium tremens. He ordered a special diet of beef tea, milk, eggs and brandy, but he did not recover in the two days of his treatment. The inquest heard Shortel had a severe drinking bout for two weeks before his death.

Theresa and Margaret Campbell arrived in Australia after the resolution of a longstanding dispute arising from an infamous incident in their home village of Ballyworkan, near Portadown in the northern Irish county of Armagh.

The father of the sisters, William Campbell, was part of a mob of at least 20 and up to 50 locals armed with guns and improvised bayonets who smashed their way into the home of landowner Thomas Pepper, threatening and evicting the man's housekeeper and her children.

Their action followed news that the ailing Pepper was leaving his estate to his decades-long servant Martha and her children, and not to his two nephews who were also among the whisky-sodden rampagers. They believed they were about to rightfully take possession of the family estate. Pepper died half an hour after the home invasion.

Scandalous accusations were levelled at Martha in the court case that followed, but she did eventually secure the title to the property years after the tumultuous home invasion. William Campbell was one of 19 people convicted of a variety of offences committed in the attack on the Pepper home.

Bad blood remained. The tenant-farmer Campbells decided to try their luck elsewhere.

In the early 1880s, with his mother dead and his father's drinking bouts becoming ever more dangerous, young Thomas Shortel was often left to fend for himself. His father was in and out of court on charges arising from his alcoholism. At the age of 14, young Tom was charged with embezzlement. An *Evening News* story on the matter described a 'dirty little boy' being brought before the court.

The allegation was that he had taken a basket containing a dozen pot plants which were the property of nurseryman Alfred Pearce. Tom had been given the job of taking the plants into the street to sell them, but he did not return with the flowers or any money.

He was found guilty and sentenced to seven days in Darlinghurst Gaol. The magistrate lamented that the city did not have a reformatory for such youthful offenders. His Worship also noted that the prisoner's father was a disreputable man and it was not to be wondered that the youngster should develop a criminal taste.

Thomas Shortel was 17 years old when his father died. He worked as a paper-selling newsboy around Sydney's Queen Victoria Building, which in those days was home to the city markets rather than the higher-end retailers of modern times. He eventually became a newsagent in his own right employing his own newsboys.

He also ran refreshment rooms on busy George Street and when he moved to a new site in Market Street, he acquired the newsagency and bookshop across the lane. The bookshop specialised in sheet music and other related titles.

The lane between the two shops offered a doorway to a rear room. This was the location of Shortel's bookmaking business, the site of the riot that preceded his departure for Canada. The laneway was well-known as a place to play Australia's most commonplace gambling game of the day, two-up. Like off-course starting-price betting on horses, it was illegal, but very widely played. The selective blindness of corrupt police ensured some profits were shared and a relatively relaxed tolerance prevailed.

Shortel's innovation in newspaper sales was the introduction of squads of children in a kind of dustcoat uniform selling papers, a card on their caps indicating which titles they carried. Some of the poor or homeless children earning a few pennies this way were provided with dormitory sleeping accommodation.

The apparent generosity had clear and enforced boundaries. Anybody trying to pilfer an extra coin here or there was vigorously pursued even as far as the local courts, just as Shortel himself had been. Youth offenders were regularly locked up in police cells for spells of a few hours.

Tom Shortel's great theft of punters' wagers on the 1903 Melbourne Cup was a scandalous betrayal of public trust. Thousands of pounds belonging to hundreds of gamblers were simply scooped up by Shortel to be used as he saw fit. The race fraud was the nadir of his depravity.

His efforts in employing poor newsboys are evidence of a gentler disposition, a clear indication of a social conscience, albeit one which also offered him chances for social climbing.

Newsboys had worked in Australian cities since the mid-19th century selling newspapers on the street in exchange for a small income of commissions on papers sold. Melbourne's newsboys started working as early as the 1840s, with Brisbane and Sydney following later.

In the late 1890s, Tom Shortel's newsboys became more noticeable as wearers of a kind of uniform. The *Brisbane Courier* noted in 1900 that 'a visitor to Sydney is at once struck with the modern method of selling newspapers introduced so successfully by Mr T. Shortel (of T. Shortel and Co.) who has some 500 boys dressed in neat white coats and smart caps with bands indicating the name of the paper sold.'

Moving into the new century, his picnic day charity initiative to support street-selling newsboys was backed by the New South Wales Premier, John See, and the state's Lieutenant-Governor, Sir Frederick Darley. It was a remarkable rise to prominence.

Every year Shortel would organise a picnic day for these children which would include a ferry trip, a well-catered picnic, and games including foot races, tug-o-war contests and other amusements. He sought and received donations from major newspapers *The Evening News*, *Australian Star*, the *Daily Telegraph*, the *Sunday Times*, *Truth*, *The Bulletin* and after some dithering, the *Sydney Morning Herald*, to cover the cost of the picnics. Food and beverage suppliers also joined in.

Tom Shortel was now directly connected to opinion-makers at the big end of town.

The events were widely reported and won high praise from those who backed the venture. They lifted the profile of Shortel as a kind and considerate man, one whose social standing had already risen through his marriage to Pauline, a classical singer and member of a respected family of German origin prominent in Sydney's artistic and intellectual life.

Newspaper accounts from the early years of the new century give a glowing picture of the admiration its fans had for the picnic day and how it had claimed a place on the Sydney calendar.

The crowd of kids taking part had blown out to as many as 600. There were mountains of sandwiches with a 1903 report describing the supply of 1,200 bags of cakes, fruit and confectionery, as well as 250 gallons of ginger beer and milk. There was also a plentiful supply of cigarettes for the older boys, lads aged 12 or 13.

The New South Wales state government's endorsement extended to supplying a ferry to take the street sellers across Sydney Harbour to Pearl Bay. Ministers gave speeches and indicated approval and funding for a plan to establish a Newsboys Institute which would offer evening classes.

Tom Shortel's connections included not only the now knighted premier Sir John See, but also the likes of band leader Lewis de Groen and other leading lights of Sydney's music milieu where his wife Pauline Süssmilch and her family were prominent.

Shortel volunteered as a fundraiser for the South Africa Day Committee, formed to establish a commemoration day to mark the service of Boer War veterans. He headed a subcommittee under the leadership of the Florence-born Dr Thomas Fiaschi, a surgeon with an international reputation who served in South Africa with the New South Wales Medical Corps, having already given service to the Italian Army in Abyssinia.

In a legal dispute over promised donations to the Committee, Shortel was represented in court by Ayrault Burns, son of the former Postmaster-General and Colonial Treasurer, John Fitzgerald Burns.

In 1902, Shortel secured the rights to print the Committee's souvenir programmes and posters. His links to publishers meant he cultivated good contacts not only in newspapers but also in printing and publishing. He secured an exclusive deal with the Royal Agricultural Society (RAS) to issue advertising material for the Royal Easter Show, Sydney's annual carnival featuring prize farm animals, produce and fairground attractions.

No doubt the fact that Sir John See was the head of the RAS at this time was not exactly a hindrance. Fiaschi was also a member of the RAS Council. Shortel's penchant for picnic day popularity would be repeated in Canada with carnival-based fundraising at Brockton Point for Vancouver General Hospital.

Fiaschi went on to be the commanding officer of the Number 3 Australian General Hospital in Lemnos during the Gallipoli campaign. The Australian War Memorial holds photographs of Australian servicemen playing soccer there away from the battlefront.

Tom was the firstborn of the Shortel children. His brother Sydney, six years his junior, was a lifelong companion. When the police started their search for Tom, they were on the lookout for Sydney too. Big brother Tom always protected his younger sibling and provided him with jobs in his gambling and tobacco businesses. Sydney did return to Australia on a trip in 1933 but died in British Columbia.

Newsboy organisations and events thrived in cities and towns all over the country up to World War I, but in Sydney they struggled to draw the financial support they enjoyed in Tom Shortel's days before 1904. The Christmas picnic did not go ahead in 1909, and newsboy strikes took place in Newcastle and Sydney.

Newsboy initiatives were still generally well-regarded, but the Shortel name was no longer part of their reputation.

CHAPTER 4
The Süssmilchs

Thomas Shortel's social rise was confirmed by his 1896 marriage to Pauline Süssmilch, the eldest daughter in a much respected family in Sydney society.

The union between the son of a working-class Irish immigrant and a daughter of a well-to-do German family committed to arts and sciences may seem unlikely, but their union lasted 23 years until Con Jones' death.

Pauline Süssmilch, known as Paula Jones in Canada, was the figure who held the family together through the trauma of scandal in Sydney and innuendo about criminal activity in Vancouver. Paula Jones remained a board member of the Con Jones Limited company after Con's death. She also took in two daughters from Con's previous liaisons.

The patriarch of the clan, Christian Bernhard Süssmilch, left his birthplace of Hamburg on the *Reiherstieg* bound for Sydney in 1856. His travel papers list his occupation as *Musikprofessor*. He quickly established himself as a leading figure in the German community and was in demand in Sydney's music world as a conductor and teacher.

He organised choirs, concerts and ensembles large and small, and showed his commitment to social causes with many performances held to raise money for charities.

When Prince Alfred became the first member of the British royal family to visit the colony in 1867, C.B. Süssmilch was prominent among the music leaders called on to take part in ceremonial events marking his presence. A concert and torchlight parade by the German community received much attention.

In 1869 and nearing his 40th birthday, he married Anna Emilie Merkle, the 23-year-old daughter of Joseph Merkle, a judge from Wurttemberg in southwestern Germany. Pauline was the second of their seven children all born in Sydney over the next 16 years.

The most illustrious of the siblings was Carl Dolphe von der Heyde Süssmilch, a scientist with a significant international reputation in the fields of physiography and geology. He was a Fellow of the Geological Society in London and a recipient of the Clarke Memorial Medal for Australian research. He was also a president of the Royal Society of New South Wales, the Linnean Society, head of the Newcastle Technical College and a trustee of the Australian Museum.

Carl Adolphe was a leading figure in the Pan Pacific Science Congress, which consistently emphasised that a knowledge of the Pacific Ocean and its peoples was essential for the economic development of the region and the peaceful co-operation of its far-flung communities.

He regularly gave lectures on Pacific issues during the 1920s, often under the auspices of the Workers Educational Association.

Pan Pacific ideas were an expression of regional awareness, though still not fully in the mainstream of intellectual circles dominated by European and American thought. His pan-Pacific activity regularly took him to Vancouver and stays with his sister and her family.

Pan Pacific ideas were evidently shared by other members of the family. When the fourth conference of the left-leaning Pan Pacific Women's organisation was held in Vancouver in 1937, one of the social events was a celebratory evening of folk dancing. Australian conference delegate Isabel Randall-Colyer, writing in the *Sydney Morning Herald*, described the happy gathering at 'the pretty Spanish hacienda of Mr and Mrs Harold Jones.'

In his retirement, Carl Süssmilch worked as a volunteer for the Crippled Children of New South Wales.

Pauline was a gifted pianist regularly invited to play in Sydney at private gatherings and charity fundraising events. Her sister Emma Emilie was the most highly praised artist of the siblings, one of the city's singing stars of her time, and a student at the Königliche Hochschule in Berlin where she studied for two years under Meta Lippold and celebrated singer Adolphe Schulze. Emma was admired for her command of a broad range of music but had a special skill in singing German lieder.

Her brother Emil Süssmilch was also a well-regarded singer. Emil and Emma often performed together in the later years of the 19th century. In the 1920s, they sang together in a performance broadcast by ABC Radio.

Pauline Süssmilch often shared the bill with illustrious performers on Sydney's stages. One of them, Alice Charbonnet, was known as one of the singing teachers of operatic diva Nellie Melba. After singing and teaching in Sydney and Melbourne, Madame Charbonnet was appointed as the music critic of Parisian publication *La Nouvelle Europe*. She was also the mother of Sydney-born Hollywood star Annette Kellerman.

Kellerman was a box office attraction in Australia and North America. The 'Australian Mermaid' is credited as the creator of synchronised swimming and is remembered as the first person to appear naked in a Hollywood movie, 1916's *Daughter of the Gods*.

A 1905 *Sydney Morning Herald* report on the activities of Australians in London notes Emma Süssmilch's spell in Berlin, a concert she gave in London, and another due in Birmingham. She was to return to Sydney via North America with further concerts already arranged at St. Paul, Minnesota and, of course, Vancouver. A three-week holiday in Fiji included another scheduled performance.

All of the musical Süssmilchs shared the stage with renowned singing couple Phillip Newberry and French-Canadian soprano Emily Spada among their hundreds of performances before and after the turn of the 20th century. The couple visited Paula in Vancouver, but their popularity and financial fortunes dipped drastically in later life. They died in poverty in Brooklyn within two weeks of each other in 1936.

Music remained central to the home life of the Jones clan in Canada. A family friend from Sydney, Isabel Ramsay, wrote in a letter published in the *Sunday Times* newspaper that her trip to Vancouver showed that Pauline had successfully inculcated her love of music in her children.

She remarked that they formed a small chamber music ensemble among themselves and went on to say that the Jones home was a place of reunion for noted musicians passing through the city. Con Jones himself was known to sing songs at less-formal social events in Sydney and continued his singing in Canada.

The Süssmilch family maintained a consistent level of contact between Vancouver and Sydney. Carl Süssmilch's Pan Pacific work allowed him to drop in on his sister. Emma, by then Mrs Horace Bately Allard after her marriage in 1909, was also a guest while Pauline's brother Franz travelled with the Jones family group on their initial migration across the Pacific in 1904. He died in Vancouver a couple of months before Con in 1929.

There were also visits to Sydney from the Canadian-based family, although Con, no doubt keen to stay away from the law, never set foot in Australia again.

The family connection lapsed with the death of Paula Jones in 1950. The last survivor from the original family unit transplanted from Sydney in 1904 was Felix. He accompanied his mother to Australia in 1930, the year after Con's death, but had no continuing relationship with any of the Süssmilchs in Sydney and did not return.

CHAPTER 5
Pacific Soccer League

The Pacific Soccer League envisaged by Con Jones in 1908 was a bold enterprise aimed at creating a new and higher-level playing standard through bigger crowds and professionalism.

He hoped one competition involving teams from the Canadian and the United States Pacific coast could also rise above the parochialism that tied up grander ideas in red tape and petty jealousies.

It did produce professional games and earned Jones praise in the United States, his first international recognition.

Con Jones succeeded in planting his ambitious league's flag in the ground, but the league failed in its original form. The present-day Pacific Coast Soccer League includes teams from the two countries and although it is fundamentally different to his original design, it acknowledges Con Jones' creation as its foundation.

Jones believed that stepping beyond localism and into the bigger world of regionalism would cast the net further to increase investment in the game and attract greater support from sports fans.

Critics warned that the time had not yet arrived for the league. They thought a competition spread over a large geographical area with eight or nine playing centres would create organisational problems that would kill its viability. Some were also wary of a structure which would raise Jones' power and reduce their own local authority.

Jones believed the prevailing attitude amounted to passively sitting still and accepting mediocrity. He thought soccer's eastern establishment was too far away to offer a chance for growth anytime soon and that a leap of faith simply had to be taken. He told the *Victoria Daily Colonist* in an interview that expansion was required if 'soccer football would ever obtain the hold on the people of the Pacific coast that it had in the Old Country'.

He believed there would be support from clubs in Vancouver, Nanaimo, Ladysmith, Victoria and across the border in Seattle. He thought there could be interest too from Tacoma in Washington state and Portland, Oregon. If they could put up a team strong enough, they would be welcomed.

'I'm in favour of making it international in its scope, and the same is the opinion of all Vancouver sportsmen. At any rate give them all (the U.S. teams) an opportunity to make a running for the pennant if they have the pluck to try.'

Participating teams had to pay a $10 registration fee as well as 5% of all gate takings. Jones would award a $100 silver trophy to the league champions.

In the end, and despite a major push to cultivate Californian support, the local all-star side Seattle United from Washington state was the only United States team to accept the invitation. The relatively isolated soccer advocates in northern California saw opportunities for advancement, but shaky finances and a change in California state leadership killed the cross-border relationship.

Jones organised and paid for an All-California selection to tour British Columbia in April 1909. Their players, according to his partner Will Ellis, were all of English and Scottish origin. The initiative drew effusive praise from California Football Association secretary Sam Goldman, who travelled to Canada as the manager of his state's team.

The *Spalding's Guide* has Goldman insisting that great credit should be given to 'Con Jones, President of the Pacific Coast Football League who financed the project privately, and Mr Will Ellis, secretary of the same league who had charge of affairs in B.C. The untiring efforts of these two gentlemen are worthy of the highest commendation and all California soccer enthusiasts sincerely thank them for the boost this tour has given the game here.'

Goldman went on to lavish further praise for the hospitality shown in Vancouver, which included launch excursions, men-only smoking concerts and placing the National Sports Club at their disposal.

'The history of association football in America would be incomplete without the mention of Messrs Con Jones and Will Ellis, and any community should be proud to have as citizens such true sportsmen as these gentlemen are.'

A British Columbia All Stars selection made a return trip to California, again paid for by Jones.

The celebration of their grand cross-border shared cause did not last long. The league struggled through its first season and it was decided to delay the start of a second season until 1910. The venture failed to take off. Jones persevered in 1910 even though he had just two Vancouver teams, the Rovers and the Callies.

Changes in the leadership of the California Football Association also reduced Goldman's status and raised the position of southern California in relation to the north. The Pacific Soccer League was no longer a priority.

The League at least provided what esteemed Canadian soccer historian Colin Jose described as the first professional game to be played in Canada when Callies defeated Rovers 3–0 at Vancouver's Recreation Park in March 1910.

The blue and gold colours of California were the first international shirts seen in British Columbia. They were followed by a Corinthians side led by former England captain Christopher Wreford-Brown. The British Columbia leg of their tour was overseen by Jones.

The third version of the radically reorganised Pacific Coast League started in 1930, acknowledging its origins by naming the winner's prize as the Con Jones Memorial Trophy.

CHAPTER 6

George Arthur Parker – King of Empire Football

The first big-time promoter in the new age of international football touring was George Arthur Parker, a man who also influenced Con Jones. Parker was the man behind Corinthians' trips to South Africa starting in the 1890s, the association game's first inter-continental tours.

London's Corinthians club was the most famous amateur side in the world from the 1890s into the new century. The club cultivated an image of soccer evangelists going abroad to spread the football gospel, while embodying amateurism and the very best English values of fairness and sportsmanship.

Questions about the purity of their mission arose from the start.

Given his impact on the game, Parker is a strangely overlooked character in accounts of its history. As an amateur in the late 19th century, he played in F.A. Cup matches and in friendlies against the likes of Woolwich Arsenal and Luton Town.

His club football was mainly with amateur side Polytechnic F.C., but he also played in teams representing the London F.A. and Middlesex. He also took the field with the world's oldest continuously playing club, Sheffield F.C.

In South Africa, he was the captain of the national championship-winning Transvaal team and played for South Africa against Corinthians on the 1897 tour when he was the manager.

His book *South African Sports*, published in 1897, gives a good account of the early development of association football in that country and is perhaps the first national history of the game anywhere in the world.

In the 1890s and early 1900s, Parker was the world's leading international football tour promoter. His familiarity with the soccer cultures of English-speaking countries was unsurpassed with knowledge gleaned through his experiences in England and on the road in South Africa, the United States and Canada. He made overtures to extend his touring efforts to New Zealand and Australia, but did not succeed.

He was always referred to in print as G.A. Parker and known to his friends by his schoolboy nickname – 'Gap'. At London amateur side Polytechnic F.C., he played mainly as a right winger but also as an inside forward and right-sided half-back and full-back.

Polytechnic's rising status in the 1890s was attributed by the school's in-house magazine to Gap Parker, the captain. Parker was also rising as a figure in the game's politics, being elected to the committee of the London F.A. in 1890. Other London officials were F.A. President Lord Kinnaird, F.A. Secretary Fred Wall, the captain of the first F.A. Cup winning team Charles Alcock, and Corinthians founder N.L. 'Pa' Jackson. Kinnaird played alongside Parker as a guest at Polytechnic.

Parker wrote about football for the *Polytechnic Magazine* and admired 'Pa' Jackson's initiative in starting the *Pastime* sports journal in 1893. Jackson was on hand at Southampton in 1897 to wave off the Corinthians players for their trip to South Africa, having appointed Parker as the tour manager.

Parker was already known in South Africa as captain of the Wanderers club and honorary secretary of the South African Football Association. It was his invitation letter to Jackson in 1895 that set the wheels in motion for a tour. Corinthians' first South African trip was a success, but there were growing doubts about the purity of the club's claims to be at the forefront of amateur values unsullied by financial considerations.

There were questions about the size of match-fee guarantees demanded by Corinthians for some games and the big expenses bills of the players that critics implied were padded out to conceal their real role as de facto payments.

The second South African tour in 1903 again had Parker as manager and went well on the field, but with another wave of comments that the exemplars of amateur values were not quite as clean as they would like them to be seen. *Sporting Life* in London noted players 'returned with fatter purses than they took out'.

Parker suffered a disastrous personal episode in 1899 with illness causing him to lose his eyesight. He returned to London from Cape Town to undergo treatment at Westminster Ophthalmic Hospital, which restored some vision.

His old friends staged benefit matches for him and his dependent family, featuring many prominent players.

It was reported that he had invested and lost his money in South Africa starting up a sports-only newspaper, *Sports and Pastimes*, an echo of Jackson's paper *Pastime*. Despite the benevolence of his old pals, he wound up facing bankruptcy proceedings.

He gave evidence that he had borrowed hundreds of pounds from Quintin Hogg, his immensely wealthy mentor from his Polytechnic days. The Polytechnic was founded by Hogg and went on in stages to become the present-day University of Westminster. Hogg was also a football man and played for Scotland in two of the five unofficial international games preceding their first official match in 1872.

The bankruptcy court heard Parker hoped to repay his debts with money earned arranging a football tour to the colonies by an English team. This was the 1906 Corinthians trip to the United States and Canada.

North America became his new focus as innuendo over the division of revenues meant he was not a candidate for the third and last South African tour in 1907. Parker's bankruptcy court evidence clearly shows that he saw the Corinthians trip as a way to generate income for himself.

The guarantor of the 1906 Canada and USA tour was the London newspaper *The People*. After its completion, Parker emerged as a representative of *The People* bearing a trophy as a gift to be awarded to the champion team of Canada. The People Shield, usually referred to as the *People's Shield*, was the beginning of the relationship between Parker and the man who on home turf would develop his own ideas about touring and national championships, Con Jones.

Parker stayed in the newspaper business but faded as a sports promoter. In the 1930s, he still held an international role for *The Daily Mirror* and was seen enjoying an international rugby match in New Zealand while on a personal tour which took in Australia.

A selection of images of the newsboys outing from 1897.
Illustrated Sports and Dramatic News 11-10-1897, held by the Dictionary of Sydney.

Jones' confidant, advisor and partner, New Zealand Will Ellis. This picture shows him at a match of the Vancouver Lacrosse Club, where he was the honorary secretary. *Vancouver Lacrosse Club annual report 1906.*

Con Jones, second from right, front row. George A. Parker, fourth from right, front row, Jim Adam in playing kit behind Con Jones. *John Fuller collection.*

Con Jones behind the victorious Vancouver Celtics team in 1910.
Con Jones scrapbook held in the John Fuller collection.

British Columbia and California players along with Con Jones, Will Ellis and Californian official Sam Goldman. *Spalding's Guide 1910.*

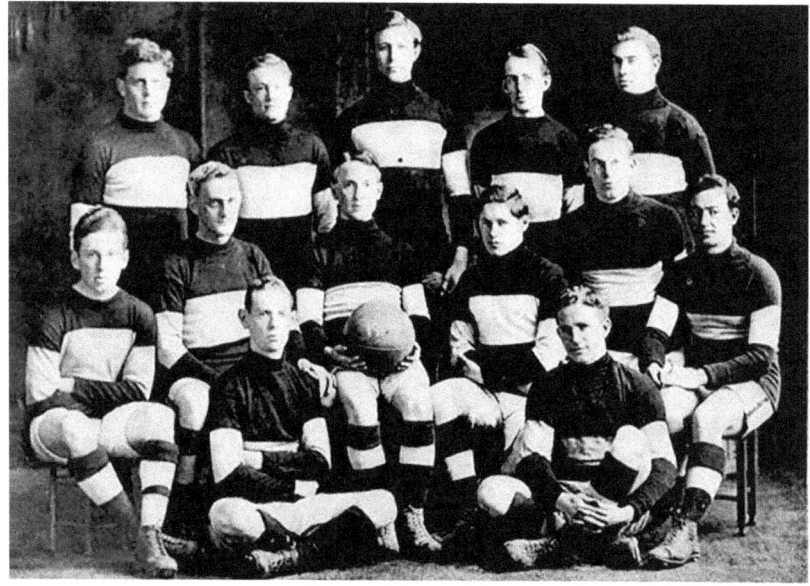

Springfield, 1911. Douglas Lamb second from right, middle row. Jack Storr sitting on the ground, front row left. Lamb went on to be a leading figure in the Canadian Olympic movement. Storr captained Southern Tasmania.

The football ground at Con Jones Park. *British Columbia Soccer Association.*

Con and Paula Jones with their four sons and Con's older daughter Amy Jones, 1914. *John Fuller collection.*

The Canadian squad visiting Adelaide, Australia, with manager Jim Adam wearing a suit in the top right of the picture. *Adelaide Register, 11 July 1924.*

Louis Denison Taylor was a populist, labour-friendly Liberal who was elected eight times mayor of Vancouver. He faced corruption accusations and was a friend of Jones. This photo shows him kicking off a match at Con Jones Stadium in 1927.

Probe Estimates Revenue of Club $155,000 Yearly

Probe May Be Out of Morgue By Voting Day

But Officials Will Not Even Make a Guess.

What will be the length of the present police enquiry by Commissioner W. A. Macdonald?

The question brings shrugs and bland, puzzled smiles from those in charge of the investigation.

After the close of Wednesday's session, R. L. Maitland, K.C., the commission counsel, would not even venture a guess. He's making as good time as possible, but . . . and the same day he had told the Commissioner that he proposed to go deeper, much deeper, than the Tucker report.

Brunswick Manager Is Witness Before Enquiry.

HAS 32 TABLES

Hon. W. A. Macdonald and R. L. Maitland, K.C., commissioner and counsel respectively of the current police enquiry, this morning whetted their knowledge of stud poker and seven-tied pete on the broad Scottish brogue evidence of Robert Mercer, licensed manager of Brunswick Sports Club.

Mercer, whose salary is $40 a week, was called on to explain to the commission the mode of play in the three-storey premises near the City Hall, where thirty-two card tables are estimated to produce a goodly portion of yearly gross earnings that the commissioner estimated at $155,000.

Thomas B. Jones, one of the Jones brothers, who form the directorate of the Brunswick Club,

Revelations about the revenues of the Brunswick Club, 1936.

Street signage on Hastings Street, Vancouver, in 1946, one of many to survive long after the death of Con Jones. *Vancouver Archives.*

Part of the Jones tobacco shops paraphernalia. *Vancouver Archives.*

CHAPTER 7
The People Shield

The plan hatched by Con Jones and Will Ellis to use the People Shield in the service of the national team was an audacious move with the potential to transform the game in Canada.

Jones and Ellis directly addressed the issue of what it is to be a national team. They proposed that national team selection should result from performances in competition rather than as the result of the horse trading of soccer administrators. The best players should make up the team regardless of where they came from. This would be better than a cherry-picked group reflecting region-by-region representation.

The two men seized on the Shield and talked up its status as a de facto national club championship. They had a vehicle for their plan to create a genuinely meritocratic selection system. It was a move in tune with the times as national teams and organisations grew in prominence.

The People Shield tournament included teams from several provinces and was promoted by its backers as a de facto national title. However, it never reached that lofty target.

The People Shield was eventually displaced by the best claimant on the status of national title, the Connaught Cup. President Fred Barter was reported to have told the 1913 annual general meeting of the Dominion of Canada Football Association of the Shield's sad fate. It was in a pawn shop in Calgary for the sum of $400.

The Shield's third edition was held in British Columbia in 1908 after the arrangement was confirmed in a letter from the trustee of the Shield – the promoter now working as a journalist for *The People*, G.A. Parker, in November 1907. Only teams from Ontario and Quebec took part in the 1906 first edition with Toronto Thistles beating Dundas 1–0 in the final. The once-blind Parker refereed this first decider.

The following year saw sides from four provinces compete, with Calgary Caledonians lifting the trophy after a 1–0 victory over Winnipeg Brittania. The sole goal scorer, young defender Andy McLean, was still around in the twilight of his career to be part of the Canadian tour of Australia in 1924. He played in all six of the full international matches and was sent off in the last of them, a 1–0 loss in Adelaide.

A committee was formed to arrange what was hoped to be a competition with nine teams, four of them from British Columbia. Con Jones headed a five-member organising committee which included his colleague Will Ellis, and Jim Adam from Ladysmith. In 1924, Jim Adam would be the manager of the Canadian national side's tour of Australia. Ellis refereed the final of the third People Shield.

In March 1908, Jones and his partner Ellis sent a letter to provincial soccer administrations across the country proposing a radical plan to recruit and send a team representing Canada to the Olympic Games to be held later in the year in London.

Jones and Ellis were so strong as advocates of a Canadian presence in the football competition that other provinces suspected their real intention was to try to dispatch a British Columbia team to the Games. It seems they did consider this idea as a contingency if their main idea did not win support from other provinces.

They proposed that a committee be formed to watch People Shield games and pick the best players to play a trial against British Columbia's star players that were also playing in the Shield. From this trial, a best 11 could be selected. This team would then head east towards the ship to take them to England, but other matches were to be played along the way.

The Jones and Ellis letter envisages a game against an Alberta select in Calgary. If any players there looked worthy of a place, they could be included in the squad. Although they thought players from top side Calgary Caledonians would already have reserved a spot through the People Shield, a match could be played in Alberta to give others in the province a chance to shine.

The rolling caravan of players might then face Saskatchewan in Regina, Manitoba in Winnipeg, Ontario in Toronto and finally Quebec in Montreal. By the end, 'Canada would have a thoroughly representative team of some seventeen or eighteen players who could go to England and be a credit to the

Dominion.' The gate revenue taken along the road would go towards covering the expenses of the team.

Soccer leaders in Alberta made their own moves to win the favour of the *People* in jockeying for the right to stage Shield matches. Will Ellis demolished their case set out by one of the founders of the powerful Caledonian club in Calgary, Dr George Ings.

The Jones/Ellis plan was clever even though it is easy to see the many logistical problems they would have to overcome. What about travel and accommodation bills? What about some level of recompense for the players? Would compensation compromise their amateur values? Which players would be available for this mini-marathon?

A mechanism for national selection which was dependent on performances at the highest level that the domestic game could provide would result in a squad of genuine quality. The knowledge that the Shield could be a platform for a place at the top table and a place at the Olympics would surely motivate players.

However, the initiative came to nothing. The financially strapped Canadian Olympic Games Committee opted to endorse only teams or individuals it believed had a genuine chance to win medals. The country's footballers were held to be short of the standard required to have a chance of reaching the podium.

In any case, other provinces saw Jones' ambitions as an irritant upsetting their own status and as something worth holding in check.

Con Jones was not discouraged. International football remained at the head of his ambitions.

CHAPTER 8
Don't Argue – Con Jones in Vancouver

Canada did not have much of a profile in turn-of-the-century Sydney, but the name of the country did have some visibility through local geography and café menus.

Canada Bay on the Parramatta River is ten kilometres west of the Sydney CBD. Prisoners from the Lower Canada Rebellion of the 1830s – 58 French Canadians and two Irish men – were despatched to Australia. The men collected oyster shells from the bay to make lime for the construction of Parramatta Road, the major traffic artery west from the city.

Around Sydney, cafés advertised 'Canadian meals' heavy with pancakes.

As far as soccer was concerned, one sarcastic press backhander from 1909 stands out. Sports paper *The Arrow* noted that 'South Coast centre half Pallier is an old Canada representative. His movement at times on Saturday indicated that he might have been connected with the lumber trade.'

One of Australia's all time greats, James 'Judy' Masters captained the national team against Canada in 1924. His father Alexander was a coal miner born in Nova Scotia who emigrated to Australia

Australia's most obvious presence in Vancouver was implied rather than stated. Any visitor to the city in the 1920s and 1930s was likely to see the 'Don't Argue' street advertising of Con Jones' tobacco shops.

The full message was 'Don't Argue – Con Jones sells fresh tobacco'. The slogan started in newspaper adverts before World War I and became ubiquitous around town as the tobacconist's shop empire stretched close to 20 premises by 1920.

Con Jones was among the first to introduce neon signage to Vancouver, a city which became famous for neon with up to 19,000 illuminations in the peak years of the 1950s. A campaign then began against the lights which were increasingly seen as tawdry and intrusive.

The full logo has a clear Australian history. It depicts a smiling, vaudeville-style, bowler-hatted man facing the viewer with one hand held up to the face of another man, depicted in profile. It seems to be a direct rip-off of an image used by prominent Australian business Hutton's Smallgoods with the slogan 'Don't Argue – Hutton's Hams Are The Best'.

The Don't Argue imagery was featured on tokens in Jones' pool halls. The tokens were used as a form of exchange for trivial purchases in the Jones establishments but could have been used for grander outlays. The use of tokens was not unknown in other businesses, but the silver-coloured Jones tokens are probably the best known. They have been exhibited in a Bank of Canada currency display.

The catchphrase certainly served the purpose of promoting Con Jones in Vancouver and is perhaps the best remembered Jones legacy in his adopted city. The expression was used to emphatically cut short an opposing view and was used in political cartoons. The slogan became so pervasive that long after the tobacco stores disappeared, Don't Argue remained part of Vancouver's commercial vocabulary. 'Don't Argue' has been the name of a café and pizza restaurant.

In Australia, a 'Don't Argue' is a straight-arm fend-off by an opponent while carrying the ball and is used in the Australian Rules game as well as the rugby codes. Jones' commercial appropriation of the slogan was completed by securing copyright over the logo in Canada.

Jones' employment of others of Australian extraction brought another stream of influence into Vancouver life. He used two prominent Australian-born architects, Henry Holdsby Simmons and Hugh Astley Hodgson, in what became a considerable construction programme. Some of their buildings were later protected by heritage orders.

The stadium in Con Jones Park in east Vancouver was designed and built by Simmonds and opened in 1921. The compact ground provided seating for 6,000 spectators with standing room available for another four or five thousand.

Simmonds also designed the luxurious Jones home on Connaught Drive in upmarket Shaughnessy. Even the plans for the lavish house and its projected construction cost received newspaper attention in the early 1920s.

The Vancouver Heritage Foundation describes the gambrel-roofed home's interior as 'stunningly original' and the *Vancouver Sun* published a photographic display of the house and its gardens.

It has six bedrooms and five bathrooms, with 650 square metres of internal space, a lower- floor billiard room and an adjacent tennis court. It has been included in a Vancouver heritage walking tour of 1920s architecture. The house has sold for millions of dollars. The stated value at the time of construction was $22,000.

Simmonds was also responsible for the Art Deco pavilions at the sprawling Pacific National Exhibition grounds in Hastings Park. The PNE is best known for its fairground but was also used as an internment camp for Vancouver's significant Japanese population during World War II. The PNE was built across the road from Con Jones Park in the mid-1920s.

Hugh Hodgson was also responsible for PNE building designs and started his work for Con Jones as early as 1911 with the Brunswick billiard parlour on nearby Hastings Street.

Although Simmonds' Australian background is well-acknowledged in Canada, Hodgson's Australian links are rarely mentioned. He was born in Brisbane to English immigrants Samuel and Margaret Hodgson. His father was a member of the colonial Queensland parliament before leaving Australia when Hugh was six years old.

Henry Simmonds' architectural passion was the movie theatre, an interest he shared with Con Jones. The most famous of his many cinemas of the 1920s and 1930s was the art deco Stanley Theatre completed in 1930.

The interior is dominated by a gilded dome and soaring arches with stylised light fittings and ornamentation. Echoes of these features are prominent in the Jones family home.

Simmonds and Hodgson went into business together in the 1920s and created not only the Stanley Theatre but also the greatly admired Olympia and Majestic theatres. During the First World War, Con Jones presented films at the Orpheum Theatre to raise money for the welfare of Canadian soldiers.

Jones promoted fad recreations in downtown Vancouver including an indoor golf course and a place to play the confected game of pushball. Newspapers printed advice on how to play.

He also produced his version of 'football pools' competitions in the early 1920s, shortly after the phenomenon took off in Britain. The score predictions were on English football matches with forms to be lodged through Jones' tobacconist outlets.

The games projected a general feeling that Jones' initiatives represented fun and good times, whether in competitive sport or novelty amusements.

The Jones home was always a place of music. Visiting artists were welcomed and the family members played and sang, including Con Jones who took his vocal training seriously.

Their family friend Francesco D'Auria was a musical figure of considerable standing, having been conductor for the North American tour of the great soprano Adelina Patti in the 1880s and a leader in the establishment of a symphony orchestra in Toronto in the 1890s.

Patti had been praised by composer Giuseppe Verdi in 1877 as 'perhaps the finest singer who ever lived' and 'a stupendous artist'. D'Auria settled in Vancouver in the same year as the Jones family and was a prominent member of the city's music community as a teacher. Con Jones was referred to in a local paper as an advanced pupil of Signor D'Auria.

Con Jones became a major force in Vancouver's sporting and cultural life whose presence was evident in buildings, promotions, events and charitable fundraising.

CHAPTER 9
Con Jones, Lacrosse and More

Con Jones launched himself into the world of Vancouver sport and leisure as soon as he arrived in Canada. He established a profile in every sport he could and quickly built a network of contacts which served as the foundation of his prominence in both sport and business.

Within six months of his arrival, Jones offered a gold medal to the winner of the British Columbia Amateur billiards championship at the Union Billiard Saloon. He took up a position as the boss of the English Bay Bathing and Athletic Club the following year. He moved the English Bay setup to east Vancouver as the National Club.

In 1907, he was offering a substantial purse of $2,000 for a boxing bout as well as managing British Columbia's middleweight champion, Joe Summers.

He promoted boxing and wrestling in his earliest days, and linked with soccer, cricket, golf, swimming, cycling, rugby and other sports in his first Canadian decade. The first to make him known to the whole country was lacrosse.

This was also a sport he came to dominate through his ability to outspend others, making him a hero to some and a villain to others. The Vancouver Lacrosse Club's victory in the Minto Cup in 1911 made the team de facto Canadian champions. It cemented Jones' identification with Vancouver and big money sport.

The key to Vancouver's success was an extraordinary and unprecedented splash of cash by Jones to recruit top players from the east. The biggest of them all was lacrosse and ice hockey star Edouard 'Newsy' Lalonde. Jones offered Lalonde $5,000 for one season, around three times his hockey salary at the Montreal Canadiens. Another recruit, Billy Fitzgerald, got $3,500 for the season. The signing of Lalonde was an earthquake in Canada's sporting world.

Lalonde was ultimately inducted into the Hockey Hall of Fame in 1950 and the Lacrosse Hall of Fame at its inception in 1965. Despite the controversies around Jones' time in lacrosse, he was also inducted in 1965.

Vancouver drew crowds of over 10,000 for big matches in this period with goal-scoring ace Lalonde a huge hit and the key drawcard at the turnstiles.

Big-money success drew plenty of strongly favourable comments in his hometown, but his move a year earlier to fire four players who went on strike for more money received a lukewarm response. His instinct for absolute control was clear. He put up the money and he called the tune.

Jones was a persistent disruptor in the world of lacrosse. His presence was particularly resented by supporters of Vancouver's perennial rivals, the New Westminster Salmonbellies. In 1909 the *Daily News* was voicing its objections to Vancouver press support for the Australian interloper.

'We wonder over here (New Westminster) who Con Jones is, and where he comes from, and where he was a couple of years ago, when lacrosse was played here, and whether he ever saw a lacrosse game before last year. If Vancouver objects to New Westminster's continued reference to 'Con' Jones, then let them begin to stop their sycophantic manner of writing about him.'

A more sympathetic voice at *The Western Call* ran a story under the headline *Con Jones The Philanthropist* which praised his help for others, made several mentions of his Australian antecedents, and claimed that he arrived from Australia 'with only moderate means'.

The regular pre-season Con Jones trips east which preceded the start of the campaign became part of the rhythm of the year and the target of some ribbing, especially his penchant for big-talking. The *New Westminster News* ran some verse under the heading of 'Con Jones' Old Song'.

Con Jones of Vancouver is back from the East
With his old spring song.
Vancouver sportswriters are having a feast
With his old spring song.
Their hopes mount as high as the blue of the sky
Con's team will be out for do or to die
And the future's as sweet as a blueberry pie
With his old spring song

Shortly after the Minto Cup victory, *The Hedley Gazette* evoked Shakespearean doom to condemn Jones and his win-at-all-costs approach. The paper edited Banquo's lines from *MacBeth* to dismiss him with disdain. 'Thou hast it now: king, Cawdor, Glamis all, thou playedst most foully for it.'

The *Gazette* went on to say that should an eastern team swoop down and carry the Cup back with them, 'Con Jones and his aiders and abettors would merit some tar and feathers at the hands of the people of B.C.'

During a dispute over match cancellation, contracts and the eligibility of players, the vitriol flowed again.

The *New Westminster News* continued the attack on Vancouver's lacrosse kingpin, demanding that 'Con Jones be relegated to the scrapheap of discredited sportsmen. The Vancouver public have been hoodwinked. They are being hoodwinked at the present time and yet many of them don't know it because some of the sports writers of Vancouver owe Jones too much to say anything against him.'

Jones certainly knew the value of maintaining good relations with key press contacts and cultivated them just as he had with his newsboy programme in Sydney. When he travelled east on his springtime trip of 1913 to deal with lacrosse matters, he took along *Vancouver Province* sporting editor Jimmy Hewitt as an advisor.

Jones' losses on lacrosse in 1912–13 led to match cancellations and players complaining about unpaid wages – all actions which had a flow-on effect for other teams. Jones subsequently resigned from the B.C. Lacrosse Association and left the sport.

The Week lamented the dilemma for lacrosse with the view that 'the man who ran it on to the rocks has now deserted the ship'. The *New Westminster News*, deriding the 'Canadian kangaroo', observed that Jones had consistently lost money on the game for two years.

Giving evidence in a court case brought by four players trying to claim unpaid wages, Jones confirmed his financial losses. 'My expenses for the year 1911–12 season were $31,000 and I could not see enough in it to justify me in making any contracts for the whole season. It cost me $7,000 when the New Westminster team refused to come over here to play and I was determined that I was not going to put myself in such a position again.'

Jones defended the broken contracts charge by arguing that he had agreed to pay players $50 per week rather than offer a salary for the season as they claimed. He was back in the game not much more than a year after his withdrawal, but the combination of World War I and the growth of ice hockey made lacrosse struggle.

At the War's end in 1919, the *Daily News* quoted Jones in Toronto declaring, 'Lacrosse is a dead end on the coast as it is here. And while I am going to make a try to get in the hockey ring I cannot but admit that soccer presents the great field for my future sporting activities.'

Professional ice hockey was now booming all over the country including British Columbia. Brothers Frank and Lester Patrick arrived from the east and formed the Pacific Coast League. They built enclosed ice rinks in Vancouver and Victoria. The Vancouver facility provided seating for 10,000 spectators.

The league started with three British Columbia teams but expanded to include Portland and Seattle by 1915. The model for soccer envisaged by Jones worked for ice hockey – a regional competition provided rising standards and an entrée to big national competition. The region was not restricted by national dividing lines and crossed the border to big population centres in the USA. Good stadiums proved to be popular with fans used to dealing with fickle weather.

Jones' sporting investments were major outlays but were no match for the scale of the Patrick brothers' hockey plans.

These developments weren't the end of lacrosse by any means, but the flamboyant, big-money professional game backed by Con Jones was over. Lacrosse would never again hold the public's attention in the way it did before the War.

CHAPTER 10
Con Jones the Pirate and his Swashbuckling Mates

By the time World War I arrived, Con Jones had become a figure on the sporting landscape whose fame had spread far beyond the West Coast. In 1913, the *Montreal Star* provided a profile of the brash newcomer for its East Coast readers.

Jones is a 'gentleman who has done more to keep the sporting pot a-simmering and a-boiling than probably any other individual in this country of recent years'.

The unnamed writer wonders why there are endlessly warring factions in practically every branch of sport and why 'a Moses does not arise to lead the way to peace and quietness and keep them there for some little time at least'. He playfully laments the burden of journalists called on 'to dictate another chapter in the everlasting fight which seems to be the principal characteristic of Canadian sport'.

The dream of tranquillity is dismissed as the article goes on to say that since 'this sketch has to deal with Con Jones the word peace is best omitted'. He is a 'lacrosse magnate, a sort of lacrosse Captain Kidd as it were, a pirate who every now and again comes East and kidnaps our star players like Newsy Lalonde, tempting them into his trap with the golden bait of the alluring West, and seemingly possessing the secret of keeping them there when once he has lured them to the balmy slopes of the Pacific.'

'Con, however, is a jovial pirate, always smiling – even when attracting from our midst our best men – with his hair cut short and standing up on edge all round his head like a porcupine's quills, and in short looking anything but the sporting magnate he has made himself.'

He's described as looking like the typical father of a large family. One of his favourite pastimes is to go out on long bike rides with his four sons. 'Among Mr Jones' other characteristics are his love of English billiards, horseback riding, and sitting on the fence while the other magnates are scrapping, then when they have all lost their breath, reaching in and grabbing what he wants.'

The Jones profile is aimed at an East Coast lacrosse audience and does not mention soccer or any other sporting business. It mentions his family in passing, at least its male members, and paints a picture of his physical appearance and general demeanour.

He had at this point only been in Canada for a shade less than ten years, yet there is nothing about his arrival from Australia and certainly nothing about the scandalous circumstances of his departure from his home country.

'Out in his own country (the Pacific coast), Mr Jones is looked upon as a great man – as he undoubtedly is.'

'He is engaging but so sharp in his commercial word that he should not be left alone.'

'You are a good fellow all right, and some magnate at that, but somehow or other for the peace of our lacrosse minds we are just as well-satisfied when you are in British Columbia as when you are nearer the biggest Canadian city.'

In the '90s TV comedy *Seinfeld*, the character George Costanza gets a job working for the New York Yankees under the legendary principal owner and managing partner George Steinbrenner.

Costanza loves the prestige of his Yankees job but lives in fear of Steinbrenner's tantrums and arbitrary decision-making, a reflection of the boss's real-life domination of on-field matters and issuing edicts like his famous banning of facial hair on players, coaches and executives.

His reign at the Yankees lasted from 1973 until his death in 2010, the longest spell of top-level baseball club ownership in Major League history which yielded seven World Series championships.

Con Jones was never in that high-flying world of sports success, but British Columbia sports writer Cleve Dheensaw describes him as Vancouver's early century George Steinbrenner.

The endless expansion of show business and sports events created a caste of entrepreneurs keen to feed the dreams of the public. These businessmen lived in a world of grand ideas, big money and high-stakes investment. Gambling is always about risking capital for the chance of grabbing star billing or a pot of gold, with the threat of financial failure and reputational oblivion lurking for the unwary.

Con Jones was going through a firestorm of condemnation from Sydney gamblers when he left Australia in late 1903 with the loot he acquired by ripping off Melbourne Cup race punters and creating a pool of cash to start his business ventures in Canada.

In his new home, he always took care to protect his name. He cultivated reporters, newspapers and local politicians. The shady back story leading to his hasty departure from Sydney was never told in any mainstream Canadian publication. Jones preferred it this way.

This relative circumspection about what the public should know set Jones apart from more swashbuckling contemporaries like Hugh McIntosh, Ernest Shipman, and even the lower-key Billy Howe.

The desire for profit and profile did not mean that Jones and the big-spending promoters he mixed with were not genuine about their public passions. A range of sports most definitely did benefit from their private investments and new thinking on competitions, cups, tours and professionalism.

In Jones' circle, they also supported the theatre, cinemas, music and architecture.

In 1908, one Australian event changed the organisation of sports forever. Promoter Hugh D. McIntosh secured a deal for the Canadian heavyweight boxing champion of the world Tommy Burns to fight challenger Jack Johnson in Sydney. Johnson literally followed Burns from North America to Europe and Australia, accusing him of running away from his title challenge. Burns finally accepted.

From the start, the fight was portrayed in the press as a contest between races. That white champion Burns would even agree to get in the ring with a black man was regarded by many white people, especially in the United States, as an act of betrayal. Press coverage in Australia and elsewhere was drenched in the most grotesque racist language and imagery.

McIntosh secured a lease on land at Rushcutters Bay Park less than four kilometres from the Sydney CBD. He built an open-air stadium on the site which accommodated 20,000 fans for the big fight which, of course, was set down for December 26, Boxing Day.

The stadium was later famous as the venue for big pop and rock 'n roll concerts in the 50s and 60s. The vast arena was eventually covered, leading comedian Bob Hope to quip that it looked like Texas but with a roof.

This stadium deal meant McIntosh was in control of the gate money, the purse for the fighters, and the advertising. He even refereed the contest. His crucial innovation was to film the event with the highest definition cameras of the time for later exhibition in cinemas all over the world. He made a fortune.

This was far from the first boxing match to be filmed but it was well ahead of the times in quality. Multiple cameras created different angles, and a gantry was constructed to enable overhead shots.

After this, film rights were no longer peripheral add-ons, they were central to the economy and planning of major boxing events. A line can be drawn from the Burns v. Johnson fight to modern commercial haggling over broadcast and streaming rights in sport.

The final production included training footage – McIntosh charged fans for access to training too – with the first showing of the film back at the stadium just a couple of days after Johnson's crushing victory. The fight lumbered on for 14 rounds as Johnson toyed with the plucky but hopelessly outclassed Burns. The bout was eventually stopped by local police fearing for Burns' safety.

Johnson left Australia seven weeks after his famous win, not to return home directly, but to go to Vancouver. Press reports say hotels there would not give a black man and his white wife a room, world champion or not.

Johnson ended up staying at the home of George Paris, a one-time fighter who was now the in-house boxing trainer at the Vancouver Athletic Club owned by Con Jones. The Canadian Paris was also a black boxer of some note who prepared Johnson for his first post-title winning bout, an exhibition clash at Jones' club with opponent Victor McLaglen, a pugilist whose career had once taken him to Australia as a prize fighter.

However, McLaglen's real triumph was as an actor greatly favoured by Hollywood director John Ford. He won the Oscar for best actor in Ford's 1935 movie *The Informer*. George Paris became Jack Johnson's personal trainer. Tommy Burns later became Con Jones' business associate.

The biggest name in Canadian film production in the early 20th century was Ernest Shipman, remembered as 'Ten Percent Ernie' for the tariff he exacted on the wages of his employees. He blithely asserted this was appropriate for his efforts on their behalf.

Shipman produced seven feature films, moving from one location to another ostensibly to tell local stories in their place of origin, but which proved to be an efficient tactic to avoid paying his bills.

Shipman ran entertainment businesses in Toronto and New York. His introduction to Australia's sports and entertainment networks came during his trip to Australia in 1908 when he accompanied the phenomenally successful touring show *The Kelties*.

The show was an exhibition of Scottish, Welsh and Irish folkloric performances featuring lots of pipes, drums and singing. *The Kelties* was a permanently touring enterprise that had been on the road for seven years before arriving in Australia in 1907 for a three-month season. However, the troupe stayed for more than a year playing to packed crowds in big cities and smaller towns alike.

Shipman and McIntosh formed a friendship which became a business partnership. Shipman was reported to have acted as a press agent for McIntosh as the media circus swirled around the Johnson-Burns fight. This work left him with what journalists would recognise as a good contact book. He wrote letters back to Australian newspapers from New York offering news about boxing, especially boxing promotion and investment.

One letter to Sydney paper *The Star* in December 1909 said that the movie rights for a Johnson-Jeffries contest would sell for $200,000 and that McIntosh might be brought in as referee. He said there was an impression afoot that McIntosh and the National Sporting Club of London had offered $100,000 to stage the fight, but that American promoters would never agree to have the event outside the USA.

On the film rights question, Shipman reported, 'Billy Howe, of Sydney, has offered fifty thousand dollars for the Australian rights to the fight pictures provided Jeffries wins. It is understood that a capitalist of Brisbane is at the back of him.' He later goes on to describe Howe as McIntosh's representative in securing boxers for bouts in Australia.

The 'Brisbane capitalist' was most likely his friend Con Jones, protecting his anonymity in an Australian sports business venture.

Four months earlier, in August 1909, the *Daily News* reported Howe's arrival in Vancouver on the way to a successful stint coaching college rugby in California. 'Mr Howe is an old friend of Con Jones and has been associated with the sport for the past twenty years. He also took a prominent part with Mr H.D. McIntosh in presenting the Burns-Johnson prize fight.'

Howe was a prominent rugby player at the turn of the century and captained the Glebe club to the Sydney premiership in 1900. He refereed matches between New South Wales and touring opponents New Zealand and England and became an administrator with the Metropolitan Rugby Union. His success in California established his name among the sporting cognoscenti and earned him invitations to contribute articles to the American press.

Baker acted in silent films in Australia before moving to the United States as a boxing promoter and stunt coach. He taught horse-riding skills to the likes of Elizabeth Taylor, Greta Garbo, Shirley Temple and Rudolph Valentino.

These larger than life characters – 'sports' as they were known – led flamboyant, attention grabbing lives of high risk in their personal and business lives, some with terrible consequences. Ernie Shipman won and lost fortunes, married five times and was highly promiscuous. A hard drinker, he died of cirrhosis of the liver at the age of 59.

Hugh McIntosh also won and lost vast sums of money and had a reputation for hard living. When he died in London from colon cancer in 1942, he was reported to have had just two pounds to his name. Friends paid for his cremation.

Con Jones was also a big drinker but was still able to maintain a family life under the direction of his loyal wife Paula. However, two of his sons died as the result of their alcoholism.

CHAPTER 11
Will Ellis – Vancouver's New Zealander

The Con Jones push for bolder, more expansive thinking was the most disruptive force in the British Columbia soccer world in the first decade of the 20th century. Shaking up the prevailing parochialism and daring to be bigger and more adventurous was the Jones hallmark.

Proposals for the cross-border Pacific Coast League and the radical plan for a national team selection system based on People Shield performances promised fundamental shifts in football thinking.

Jones arrived in Vancouver in the dying days of 1903 and began his business and sporting life in the city in 1904. Despite his status as a newcomer, his Australian background is only lightly mentioned in the newspapers of his time.

His collaborator in these bold soccer initiatives was Will Ellis who became the secretary of the Vancouver District Football League. Ellis was also a recent arrival but his background in New Zealand was hardly mentioned at all.

One newspaper profile in 1908 referred to his support for the soccer cause in England, New Zealand, Australia, South Africa and Canada. A 1934 obituary noted his late '20s appointment to the Soccer Football Commission among his many sporting, trade and industrial achievements but did not mention his early pioneering times alongside Con Jones.

William Thomas Ellis was born in Shropshire, England in 1879, the eldest of ten children. He emigrated to New Zealand in 1899. In early 1901, Ellis enlisted in the New Zealand military and went to fight in the Boer War as a member of the Rough Riders, soldiers known for their expertise as horsemen and sharpshooters.

Private Ellis served under General Plumer who was often in charge of mounted infantry groups comprising men from a mix of colonial backgrounds, including New Zealanders and Canadians.

Ellis returned from South Africa to Wellington, the home city of the New Zealand Football Association, presided over by Arthur Gibbs, one of the great figures of early trans-Tasman football. Gibbs established clubs in 19th-century Australia and New Zealand in his long career and spoke for both countries in London. He would later be formally recognised and welcomed as a member of the Football Association Council representing the two countries.

Ellis' spell in Wellington coincided with the early days of preparation for New Zealand's first international matches against New South Wales. Discussions about how to select a national team were part of the city's football chatter.

The home-and-away tours of 1903 and 1904 saw the emergence of numbered shirts on the players of both teams. This was the first use of numbers by association football international teams anywhere in the world. New Zealand was the first ever national team to wear numbered shirts.

It was in New Zealand that Ellis began working on road construction projects. It was a line of work he continued after he arrived in British Columbia in 1902 or 1903. He eventually became a road-building contractor constructing highways and streets in B.C., California, Oregon and elsewhere.

In later times, when he is remembered at all, it is usually as the father of Marjorie 'Midge' Keeble. After Will's death in 1934, his daughter Marjorie went to London and worked for the BBC. As World War II approached in Europe, she returned to Canada and became an announcer, singer and actor for the new Canadian Broadcasting Corporation. She was the first woman to read the flagship midday news on CBC radio.

CHAPTER 12
Global Football

The Football Association celebrated its jubilee year of 1913 with immense pride and a gala banquet in London attended by football representatives from all over the world. The 50 years that followed the formation of the F.A. at the Freemasons Arms in Great Queen Street had seen an astonishing growth in the game in Britain and in all parts of the globe.

One of the founders, now F.A. President, Lord Kinnaird, was the chairman of the celebration event marking the spread of football's simple but compelling passions around the planet. This was a moment of justifiable pride in a unique sporting achievement.

FIFA chiefs Baron de Laveleye and Carl Hirschmann, Austrian coaching maestro Hugo Meisl, and the man who might be described as continental Europe's biggest player, a star of the 1912 Olympics, Denmark's Nils Middleboe, who was about to become the first non-British player to sign for Chelsea, were on a list of international guests among the 400 packed in to Holborn's restaurant.

The 1912 FIFA-run Stockholm Olympiad was the first to take on the character of a genuine international competition. It was not yet global since all eleven teams came from Europe, but FIFA took pride in its achievements in less than ten years of operation.

The F.A. saw the worldwide reach of football as evidence of British cultural success, fair play and sporting values. FIFA celebrated a football empire, the F.A. celebrated the British Empire.

In the three years before World War I, teams from around the new world affiliated with FIFA, including Canada (1912) and the United States (1913). Australia was advised by London that the Commonwealth Football Association formed in 1911 was a de facto FIFA member through its affiliation to the F.A., a full member.

The Dominion of Canada Football Association DCFA sent a telegram congratulating the F.A., expressing the view that its continuing success for all time 'is the wish of all in the land of the Maple Leaf'. The years 1912 and 1913 saw Canada strongly pursuing contacts with both FIFA and the F.A., winning support from both organisations. Australia and New Zealand had a man in London, Arthur Gibbs, now co-opted onto the F.A. Council, but not a strategy to make him useful.

There were no speeches by official representatives of either Canada or Australia at the F.A. Jubilee. However, an important figure with a good knowledge of football and a thorough awareness of both countries did speak. This was Sir Gilbert Parker, Conservative Party M.P. for Gravesend.

Newspaper accounts of the banquet night say Sir Gilbert mentioned that he had represented the county of Kent in his younger days and went on to praise the F.A. as a vast association which had conquered nearly all countries with 'the true chivalry of sport'.

Horatio Gilbert George Parker was born in Canada in 1862 and was knighted in 1902 by King Edward VII for his services to Canadian literature. He wrote scores of highly popular stories about Canadian life, many of which were made into movies in the silent era and beyond.

He arrived in Australia in 1885 and toured the country as a lecturer on literature, recited his own prose and poetry, as well as the works of Dickens, Goethe and Shakespeare. He was for a time associate editor of the *Sydney Morning Herald* and wrote many observations on Australian life published in the *Herald* under the heading *My Impressions of Australia*. After visiting all states, he released the book *'Round the Compass in Australia'* in 1891.

During World War I, Parker led a covert propaganda campaign in the United States on behalf of a British government eager to involve the Americans on the British side. Furthering the interests of the Empire was his mission in public life.

Sir Gilbert Parker's prominence as a speaker on the big night showed he was clearly a man held in high regard at the F.A., certainly higher than anyone who may have actually represented Empire countries. His speech featured in almost all British newspaper coverage of the Jubilee dinner. The other literary figure to feature was his close friend Sir Arthur Conan Doyle, the well-known inventor of the Sherlock Holmes character. Less well-known is that Doyle was a founder in 1883 of Portsmouth AFC, the city's first football club. He was also the team's goalkeeper.

Despite the presence of worldliness, there was little in London that could be described as a global vision. In general discourse away from the celebrations, there was a persistent suggestion of a coming alliance of Empire countries arranging mutually beneficial touring schedules. Nothing ever happened. The idea continued well into the 1950s.

The Olympics increasingly excited ideas about international competition, while touring offered an alternative commercial path to a more cosmopolitan world.

After the formation of Australia's national Commonwealth Football Association in 1911, both options excited Australian sports figures like Alexander Knox, Bill Howe and Stephen Lynch. From Vancouver, Con Jones was in the thick of it through active involvement not only with the Australians but also with Canada's Fred Barter, Tom Cahill in the U.S.A. and Fred Wall in London.

The F.A. Jubilee gave the game cause to reflect on its past with satisfaction. The 1912 Olympiad, still fresh in the memory, promoted a focus on football's international dimensions as the path to the future. Ripples from Stockholm reached the shores of Australia.

Nobody from Australia's football fraternity went to Stockholm, but the country's leading Olympic official E.S. (Ernie) Marks was impressed by the football he saw there and thought Australia should be involved. Marks had been an official with the Australian Olympic team in 1908 and 1912. His personal background was in athletics.

He was held in high regard in Australia and in the international Olympic community. His work in Stockholm was rewarded with an honour bestowed on him by the King of Sweden.

Marks was the guest speaker at the New South Wales Soccer Football Association's annual general meeting held at the Sports Club in Sydney at the end of 1912. He gave an account of the Olympic football tournament and shared some thoughts about future Australian teams and how they might be supported financially.

Marks proposed that a 15-member football squad should go to the 1916 Olympiad in Berlin, making football the biggest single bloc of athletes in the Australian contingent. After noting the swing towards state support of Olympic teams in some European countries, he called for a reconsideration of how top level Australian sports were financed. He proposed a system of subscriptions from the public to help underwrite the cost of Olympic participation.

Soccer now had the support of a prominent figure in Australian sport who had also brought forward a financial plan which could liberate its ambitions from the limitations of the game's crippling shortage of capital. This was an enormous opportunity for the one-year-old Commonwealth Football Association to show leadership.

World War I meant no plan went ahead.

The prevailing mood was clear. Nothing excited passions more than international competition. Despite the satisfaction of the Jubilee, the F.A. had yet to provide any path forward for its loyal and obedient member, Australia.

In FIFA's annual report, Secretary Carl Hirschman had from his base in Amsterdam invoked Australia's name in writing about the organisation's future. Tom Cahill in New York had published an account in *Spalding's Guide* about Australian plans to take part in the Olympics, a tournament which was already being run by FIFA.

Cahill credited Stephen Lynch as the author of Australia's plan to go to Berlin.

Fred Wall told Australia that he was sure an application to take part in the Berlin Olympiad would be accepted, but he counselled against joining FIFA.

The desired destination was obvious. Plotting the best course to get there was still a puzzle.

CHAPTER 13
Australia's North American Tour

Just before World War 1 Australia considered a plan to tour North America.

Newspapers carried stories about an invitation to go to the United States and Canada at the expense of an American promoter, and with a chance to play in a mooted football tournament at the Panama-Pacific International Exposition in San Francisco.

This grand plan was delivered to Australia by former New South Wales Rugby League boss Alexander Knox and seems to bear the unidentified fingerprints of Con Jones. *Spalding's Guide* editor Thomas Cahill was reported by the Australian press to have taken an interest in the idea from his new base in New York, and his wealthy St. Louis associate Wynton Barker was said to be putting up the money.

Overtures to Australia and New Zealand from North America started in 1905 but picked up from 1911, the year the Commonwealth Football Association was formed. G.A. Parker wrote to the NZFA from Canada in 1905 suggesting a tour by Corinthians, or at least by Corinthians players augmented by others from Oxford and Cambridge universities.

Parker appeared to have in mind extending the 1906 Corinthians tour of North America to the West Coast before sailing from Vancouver to the South Pacific. He may have had some contact with Con Jones and Will Ellis on this matter, since Ellis was at least one man there with a direct and recent knowledge of New Zealand.

That approach followed the collapse of an earlier proposal advanced by former *Wisden* Cricketer of the Year, Gilbert Jessop, who hatched his plan after playing against a scratch Western Australian selection in Fremantle in 1903.

The English cricket team pulled in to play on their way home at the end of an Ashes cricket tour. The game was billed locally as the first international match to be played in Australia. The cricketers won 4–0 and Jessop was one of the scorers.

The *Australasian Town and Country Journal* reported Jessop had sought a 3,000-pound guarantee for the tour project from New Zealand, a huge figure for the tiny Kiwi football economy. Jessop withdrew anyway, citing time pressures of his business life.

Parker's alternative plan also fell over. Costs, logistical problems and the availability of suitable players for such a massive undertaking meant it never really received serious consideration.

Parker made a new approach in 1911, writing from Canada to NZFA Secretary Bert Salmon asking if he would be interested in a Corinthians tour in 1912. The letter was published in newspapers across Australia and New Zealand. He asks about suitable dates, financial guarantees and gate takings. There was certainly interest, but once again nothing happened.

In September 1912, Australasia's man in London, Arthur Gibbs, was admitted to the F.A. Council, a move hailed as an opening to other Empire countries which, in the view of the *Sydney Mail*, also erected a barrier to the 'exploiter and mercenary entity', that is, the private promoter.

The more exciting news that same month was Alexander Knox's notification that while on a business trip to the United States he had been asked to pass on an invitation for Australia to tour the U.S. and Canada.

Knox's letter showed there was an itinerary already prepared for matches in Vancouver, Victoria, San Francisco, Salt Lake City, Denver, St. Louis, Chicago, Toronto, Montreal, New York, Philadelphia, Baltimore and Washington. He asserted that the proposal had taken the interest of Thomas W. Cahill.

Cahill's longtime collaborator Wynton E. Barker, labelled by *The Referee* as 'American soccer's Maecenas', would guarantee the expenses of the tour and return fares. Knox stated that the idea even had backing from the Oval Office with an endorsement from President Taft. It all seemed too good to be true.

The Knox tour information went to the one-year-old national soccer body, the Commonwealth Football Association, to be dealt with by the Secretary, Stephen Lynch. It ended up being considered by the CFA at its annual general meeting in March 1913.

But why would such an important proposition be relayed to Australia by

Alex Knox, a man with no background in soccer? The other people mentioned in despatches were Tom Cahill, Wynton Barker and finally, Stephen Lynch. The most likely link to all of them was Con Jones.

In 1912, the football community learned of Australian Olympic bigwig Ernie Marks' idea of sending a team of around 70 athletes to the Berlin Olympiad in 1916 (later cancelled due to World War I). His proposal allocated 15 slots to a soccer squad. In the *Spalding's Guide* 1913, Cahill pointed to the prospect of football at the Pan-Pacific Exhibition in 1915, noting that a tournament in San Francisco offered excellent preparation for the Berlin Games.

As editor, he ran an item about soccer in Australia by an unnamed author who was most likely Lynch. On another page, there is a photograph of Lynch with a caption which says he is the 'originator of the scheme for the representation of Australia in soccer football at the 1916 Olympic Games'. *Spalding's* praised Jones' internationally minded efforts on the Pacific coast and Cahill was aware of his attempt to use a less significant tournament to launch a push for Olympic participation in 1908. It is inconceivable that a schedule which included games in Vancouver and Victoria would be touted without the involvement of Jones.

Cahill had arranged and run tours with Barker's financial support before. Jones had by then hatched a few ideas about touring and implemented a couple – Corinthians and California. Knox was the inaugural president of the NSW Rugby League when a squad was selected to tour Britain before the end of the league's first season in 1908. Barker had financed tours.

Jones' friend Bill Howe stayed with him in Vancouver before going to coach rugby at Stanford University. While there he prepared American student players for a rugby tour of Australia. Jones, Howe, Cahill, Marks, Barker and Knox all had experience and interests in furthering football tour initiatives. Marks, Howe and Knox all previously held positions with the New South Wales Rugby Union and were known to each other.

The 2013 CFA meeting dropped the link to Knox's proposed tour of the U.S. and Canada citing 'misunderstandings' with the promoters but also mentioning voluminous correspondence.

The North American tour was another to go up in smoke. The Pan-Pacific Exhibition was a big success but, in the end, did not have a soccer tournament of any note.

The experience did open doors to new ideas. Whatever the origins of the tour plan, it obliged Australian decision-makers to think about non-British options for international success and it appears to have persuaded Thomas Cahill to take some level of interest in the Australian game.

Thomas Cahill was the greatest innovator in United States soccer in the first half of the 20th century. He established a national body for the game, successfully applied for FIFA membership on behalf of his new association, coached the first U.S. national team, took the team to Scandinavia while most of Europe fought a war, and was at the heart of efforts to start a professional league.

It is hard to say whether Con Jones and Tom Cahill maintained contact with each other, but many positions they took on the importance of international matches, tournaments, tours, and professionalism were similar. Aiming to play at the Olympics and travelling to Europe to pursue their goals were also actions they shared.

The early days of international football ended with World War I. Some prominent promoters did continue after the conflict, but the shape of the football world was changing again and many of the big names fell by the wayside.

CHAPTER 14
Trans-Pacific Australians

Con Jones was certainly a high-profile Australian figure in Vancouver, but he was just one of a stream of aspiring sports enthusiasts crossing the Pacific to prove their skills and make an impact in North America.

There were many in soccer, but their stories have been overlooked.

This wasn't any kind of organised movement. It was a trend born of the personal ambition of men who wanted to see the world and make an impression on a bigger stage. They saw themselves as isolated from the more dynamic environments of Britain and America.

Shortly after Jones took control of the Vancouver National Club, Ballarat-born champion swimmer Arthur Lamb arrived to take up a role as the physical director at the Vancouver YMCA. For Lamb, this was the first step in a Canadian career which saw him inducted into the Quebec Sports Hall of Fame and the Curling Hall of Fame. Jones was named in the original list of inductees to the national Lacrosse Hall of Fame when that institution was founded in 1966.

Although both saw the sense in extending the catchment of British Columbia-based competitions in swimming and soccer south into the United States as baseball had already done, the two men seem to have had little else in common.

Jones had always understood professionalism as a key to achieving bigger sporting objectives. Lamb was committed to the amateur cause and saw no room for professionals.

After two years in Vancouver, Lamb went to the YMCA's international sports training headquarters at Springfield College in Massachusetts, earning a B.A. in physical education in 1912. He went on to study medicine at Montreal's McGill University. During World War I, he served as a captain in France and Belgium for the Canadian Army Medical Corps.

He was an Olympic team manager in Paris in 1924 and again in Amsterdam in 1928. Lamb participated in the 1932 Los Angeles Olympiad as a member of the sailing team. He set up Canada's first university department of physical education at McGill where he taught for over 30 years.

He was involved in the organisation of three editions of the Empire Games, including the 1938 event in Sydney.

Lamb is described in the Canadian Encyclopaedia as an ultraconservative and an advocate of amateurism as 'pure sport'. His notions of purity led him to question the role of women at the top level. For him, physical exercise was a good thing, but the stresses of elite sport were not appropriate for women.

The YMCA provided state-of-the-art physical training and, as an established international organisation, work and travel opportunities for men committed to physical wellbeing, competition, and Christian social values. Studying at Springfield College was an important development step for many of the organisation's most successful trainers.

Springfield had a well-regarded college soccer team and a soccer programme which provided many hours of tuition not only in fitness, but also in technical skills and tactical set ups for attacking and defending. It is hard for modern eyes to assess the quality of the tuition, but the approach to team development looks a lot more structured than anything available to Australian domestic players in the time before World War I.

John Harlow (Jack) Storr was born in Wales in 1883 but moved to Wellington, New Zealand in the first years of the new century. He was active in a booming branch of the YMCA and played in its football team. The Wellington YMCA operated under the leadership of Secretary Harry Holmes, who had already built an international reputation as a Christian leader and fitness advocate.

Storr went to Springfield and played in its soccer team for three years with at least one of those seasons in the same lineup as Arthur Lamb. He was described by the college magazine *The Triangle* as one of the finest players to wear Springfield colours. After marrying his New Zealand fiancé Bessie Luke in London in 1911, he was appointed to a YMCA position in Paris, Ontario, in 1912 before being sent to a new posting in Hobart, Tasmania.

He continued to play for YMCA, now renamed as Corinthians, and was selected three times for Southern Tasmania against the North, effectively a trial match for the imminent interstate clash with Victoria. Storr was the captain of Southern Tasmania in the last of his representative matches. Storr and Lamb played together in the Springfield team in 1911.

His YMCA mentor, the South Australian born Harry Holmes, was the delegate of the New Zealand Football Association at the 1911 congress in Melbourne which established Australia's first national football body, the Commonwealth Football Association. Ten years later, Storr attended the meeting which re-established the CFA for the post-War world.

Holmes continued to have a role with NZFA into the 1930s, listed as the organisation's representative in the United States and Canada.

The presence of YMCA personnel at both crucial meetings in the development of soccer's structures shows how closely linked this international body was to Australian decision-making. There were other links too through two Chinese tours to Australia and the Chinese trip to New Zealand. It was Arthur Dome, the Kentucky-born physical education director for the Hong Kong YMCA, who acted as the manager of the Chinese soccer tour of New Zealand in 1927.

Jimmy Summers came from Ballarat and was a close friend of Arthur Lamb. They travelled to North America together. He was noted as a successful physical education director in New York and was appointed as the first director for the YMCA in Latin America, based in Montevideo.

Captain Summers served as a non-combatant with the Canadian Red Cross on the battlefields of France. He was sent to Kent in southeast England in 1917 to recuperate from injuries and found that his medical care was to be overseen by none other than Dr Arthur Lamb.

It was while Summers oversaw YMCA sports training in Uruguay that his colleague Juan Carlos Ceriani developed the game we now know as Futsal in the World Cup year of 1930. Although there are other claimants to the title of futsal inventor, it is Ceriani's story which has been recognised and adopted by FIFA.

The most enduring contribution of the trans-Pacific Australians was that of Darwin-born Kwanglim Kwong. He left Australia as a 12-year-old and eventually studied at Columbia University in New York where he formed and played in the Chinese Students soccer team. Thomas Cahill helped the students find opponents in the New York area.

He too worked with the Canadian Red Cross in wartime France and returned to North America to complete an M.B.A. at Harvard. In 1927, he initiated and ran the Chinese tour of Australia. He also managed the champion Shanghai club side Loh Hwa.

Although he is best known for his illustrious career as a diplomat, journalist and banker, he remained active in football.

He played in or organised soccer in the USA, France, Australia and China all before the first World Cup took place.

CHAPTER 15
Con Jones in Britain

London remained the capital of the football world for the whole of Con Jones' quarter-century involvement in the game. It was the metropolitan centre of the soccer empire.

The advent of FIFA was still some way from displacing England as the centre of football power. It was the home of what he and millions of others believed were the best players and domestic competitions in the world.

Touching its lustre was surely the key to soccer progress in Canada, and building a bridge to the heartland would make Con Jones the main man for trans-Atlantic tours and the growing commercial traffic that made it all happen.

Trips to London on either side of World War I yielded agreements with the Football Association, but neither directly resulted in teams crossing the Atlantic. War defeated the aims of his first mission to London, and the changing times in Britain and continental Europe shifted the goalposts for the second.

Con Jones' trip to London in early 1914 followed formal discussions between the Dominion of Canada Football Association and the F.A. over a two-year period.

DCFA President Fred Barter went to England for three months in October 1912 and held talks with the highest officials in football. He was reported to have been invited to a special meeting of the F.A. to 'lay before that body a Canadian view of the game and try to get two first division teams to tour'.

The *Athletic News'* football doyen J.A.H. Catton, writing as ever under the pen name 'Tityrus', noted that Barter was in close contact with F.A. Secretary Fred Wall during his English sojourn. He would go home with the news that Wall had consented to an English club side visiting Canada in 1913 and left open the chance of a second team joining them. Canada's July 1912 application to join FIFA had also been granted and the door was open to go to the Berlin Olympics of 1916.

However, the momentum for the move flagged in 1913 and Con Jones went to England in early 1914 to renew the push for a trip to Canada for two of England's elite clubs, the F.A. Cup finalists no less, whoever they might prove to be. Jones had the backing of the DCFA when he negotiated directly with Wall and won his renewed backing for the Cup Finalists to travel to Canada in 1915.

The plan was suspended but not abandoned when war was declared in September 1914.

In 1919, Canada played in the Inter Allied Games football tournament at Stade Pershing in Paris, a much bigger and higher standard event than the exhibition Olympic Games competition that delivered a gold medal in St. Louis 15 years earlier. The Inter Allied teams were from eight countries that fought during the War and were composed of players who were in active military service.

Australia's soccer-playing military men had mostly left by then, but others took part in the rugby competition.

Canada finished last in a four-team soccer group won by eventual champions Czechoslovakia. In a group-stage thriller, Canada led the United States 4-1 but went down 5-4 as the American referee suddenly found cause for a stream of free kicks and penalties.

The exposure of Canadian soldiers to soccer was referred to by Jones as he sweet-talked the English press in 1920. The *Daily Mirror* reported Jones' view that Canadian soldiers went home full of soccer as 'a sport that is to be the game of the masses in Canada even to the exclusion of ice hockey and lacrosse, two of the greatest games in the world'.

The *Yorkshire Evening Post* noted Jones' comments that the game was becoming more extensively played, but Canadians did not know *how* to play.

Con Jones arrived in London with his friend and sometime business associate Tommy Burns, the former world heavyweight boxing champion who lost his title to Jack Johnson in Sydney. Jones invited journalists to lunch at Simpson's Restaurant at the Savoy Hotel in the Strand and picked up the tab. Jones was staying at the Savoy.

The assembled reporters seemed keener to talk to Burns, travelling under his birth name of Noah Brusso, the man with the higher profile in Britain. His aim of recruiting boxers for tour bouts was well-reported.

Jones' aims were not achieved. The booming world of professional football left less time for touring, especially for the kind of long-haul trip being laid out by Con Jones. Big crowds at home provided steady streams of revenue. Relatively easy money at home made tour purses less attractive for British teams and tours were becoming more expensive in any case and ever-higher risk ventures for promoters.

Fred Wall was now saying that he could see little chance of a team visiting Canada until 1922. Jones had instructions from the DCFA that although two touring teams remained the preferred option, one team would be sufficient.

Newcastle United was the prime target. The club was wired an invitation to Canada and told that Con Jones was the DCFA representative in England. Aston Villa, Everton, Chelsea, Rangers and Celtic were also on their wish list. One by one, the clubs turned him down.

The Sunderland *Daily Echo* reported that Newcastle wanted a $5,000 guarantee for a tour which Jones intended to be for 20 matches over 10 weeks. Jones would underwrite the venture. Glasgow's *Daily Record* said he was prepared to spend up to $25,000, an increase to his original budget of $20,000, calculated at $1,000 per match.

Jones explained on his empty-handed return to Canada that the biggest problems he faced had been the British clubs' fear of players being lost to Canadian clubs and jealousy among the players who wouldn't be selected to tour Canada. He said Newcastle's board had rejected his plan by a single vote.

It was a classic media message to feed to journalists. Failure was due to the actions of others and should not be laid at his feet. The economics of the post-War professional football world were a lot different to 1913, at least for top clubs. The impracticality of an old-school grand tour was not blamed. Glasgow's *Daily Record* report says Newcastle would have accepted Jones' proposal if it was for a tour of six weeks rather than ten. Six weeks though would have meant the tourists would be less likely to spend much time in Vancouver.

Con Jones' biggest tour gambit had failed. The era of teams from the British heartland going around the world on missions to promote football as played by experts was dying. Teams might consider trips where the time away from home was relatively brief and, more to the point, clearly profitable. Professional clubs would no longer endure the risk of injury to their players on long and hectic playing and travel schedules.

Nevertheless, Jones succeeded in dealing himself into the elite level of the international football trade. He had the backing of the top level of soccer administration in Canada without ever having gone through an election process to win office. He was an entrepreneur, not a bureaucrat.

CHAPTER 16
Con Jones Stadium – Vancouver Soccer's Spiritual Home

At the end of the War, the Jones family was in crisis. Con Jones went to England to bring back his son Tom at the end of a spell of military service due to his poor health.

Thomas Jones was one of three sons suffering from the so-called 'Spanish flu' which took the lives of 50 million people around the world. His eldest son was in Toronto Base Hospital with double pneumonia, the result of his flu infection. Con Jones went to Montreal and Ottawa to apply for permission to remove his son from the hospital and transfer him to Los Angeles where he could be nursed by his half-sister Amy.

The Globe quoted Jones as saying that was the recovery plan 'if he does not die, for he is desperately ill'. At this time two other sons, Dill and Noel, were also suffering from the flu but going through their recovery under the care of their mother Paula at the McAlpin Hotel in New York. All the sons survived.

The War had extinguished most sports beyond local social levels and Jones took to raising funds to support the War effort. One conspicuous effort saw him sponsor screenings at the Orpheum Theatre to collect ticket money for soldiers' families.

The longest-lasting gift Con Jones made to soccer in British Columbia was a stadium to host important matches within Con Jones Park.

The whole venture was emblematic of Jones' business conduct. A clear public good was delivered on the back of legally questionable revenues. After Jones' death in 1929, it became clear that he had only ever paid three 1,000-dollar instalments of the ten that should have been paid to acquire the land.

Many of Con Jones' ideas and innovations did not win approval from the powers that be or simply withered for the want of public support and broader private investment. Professional sport was beyond the imagination, moral values or resources of many of his contemporaries; his new competitions were sometimes regarded with suspicion; his proactive focus on international soccer contacts was for some too daunting; a daring method of recruiting a national team was for others too challenging. At times, his ideas were simply bigger than his capacity to deliver a result.

But in Vancouver, the stadium was one initiative that quickly won support and endured the test of time. The modern British Columbia Soccer Association's website refers to the stadium as 'Vancouver soccer's spiritual home'.

The football ground opened in 1921 and remained the main soccer venue in the city for over 30 years, only losing its primacy when the 35,000-capacity Empire Stadium opened nearby to host the Empire Games, now known as the Commonwealth Games, in 1954. The far more modest Con Jones Park continued to be used until 1970. It was demolished in 1971.

The ground was designed and built by the renowned Australian architect Henry Holdsby Simmonds, opening in 1921 with seating for 6,000 and more room for standing spectators. The biggest attendance figure recorded at the ground was over 9,000. The compact construction had crowds close to the action and it was popular with fans and players alike for the boisterous atmosphere generated there.

As well as being the centre of the region's local soccer culture, the stadium was a conduit for contacts with the international game. Scottish side Third Lanark were the first international visitors, followed by Corinthians in 1924.

When the Canadian national team players came home after their epic tour of Australia via New Zealand in 1924, they were brought to Con Jones Park the next day to play Corinthians. The Canadians lost 2-1. An England F.A. team led by Stanley Matthews played a 4-4 draw there in 1950, the first time a British Columbia All Star selection had held out professional opponents.

Charlton Athletic were the first English professional club side to play there in 1937 and were followed by Newcastle United, Fulham, Tottenham Hotspur and Huddersfield Town in the '40s and '50s. Scottish giants Rangers and their compatriots Aberdeen also came to town in the 1950s, as did AIK Stockholm, Mexico's Atlas, a Northern Ireland selection and Peru's Municipal.

Con Jones bought land in Vancouver which had been owned by John Callister, a builder and developer who emigrated to Canada from the Isle of Man in 1885. Callister died in 1934 leaving his property to two nieces. When one of the women died, Ada Stevenson became the sole heir to his estate.

The stadium burned down in 1934 but was rebuilt by Jones' sons under the architectural direction of its original designer Henry Simmonds. However, when it was found that Jones had only ever paid three $1,000 instalments on the original $10,000 purchase price and had also failed to meet city tax obligations, Mrs Stevenson reclaimed the title to the park. She then donated it to the city as long as it was renamed Callister Park. It continued as a sports venue.

Surviving early photographs show matches being played on a good surface, but that situation did not last. Ever more sports and events were held there with scant regard for the requirements of soccer. There was little work done to take care of the often grassless pitch which could be hard as nails or a mudheap depending on the weather. It was sometimes covered in sand in a derisory bid to give some semblance of evenness to the surface.

When Newcastle United toured in 1949, they played the B.C. All-Stars at Callister Park the week after a rodeo. Newcastle manager George Martin described the pitch as disgraceful and remarked that had the club known its state in advance, then a trip to Vancouver would have been skipped. Martin was reprimanded for his comments by the Magpies board with director Stan Seymour putting out a conciliatory statement that the club was pleased to enjoy the hospitality of their hosts in Vancouver and all over Canada.

Despite its shortcomings as a football ground, it retained a kind of magic for generations of players and fans who cherished an atmosphere they did not find anywhere else. Callister Park remained the base for the Pacific Coast Soccer League, a competition originated by Con Jones but which changed into setups in later years which would hardly be recognisable to the League's pioneers.

Likewise, the course of history that changed the name of the old ground from Con Jones Park to Callister Park obscures Con Jones' far-reaching decision to build it in the first place. His football ground was a key to transforming the status of the game in British Columbia, especially in Vancouver.

The Jones name continued to be linked to the stadium even after Con's death. His son Noel was the manager of Con Jones Park until it was returned to the city in 1934. Another son, Thomas, was for a time the president of the Vancouver Maple Leafs professional baseball team which used Con Jones

Stadium as its home ground.

Modern Callister Park is a pleasant, passive recreational area in East Vancouver with some cherry blossom-lined pathways and a children's playground. A great place for a stroll or a summer's day picnic.

There is no information provided there on the park's history, nothing about its sporting profile, and no plaque or any other acknowledgement of Con Jones and how he reshaped this part of the city and its sports culture.

Con Jones Park is where he played his own last game. He fell ill while watching a soccer match, lost consciousness, collapsed, and never recovered. He died at home a few days later in the presence of his wife and sons.

CHAPTER 17
Canada and the South Pacific

Australia holds a permanent place in the history of Canadian soccer. The 3–2 loss to Australia in Brisbane in June 1924 is listed by Soccer Canada as the country's first ever full 'A' international match.

Ten thousand fans at 'the Gabba' in Brisbane saw Fred Linning put the guests in front before a James 'Judy' Masters-led revival looked to have secured victory for Australia at 3–1. A late Les Ford goal brought Canada back into the reckoning at 3–2, but the home side held on for a narrow win.

Australia edged the series with three wins to Canada's two, but it was widely recognised that injuries, a punishing travel schedule and a squad too small to cover such an extensive fixture list counted heavily against the visitors.

Canada played 26 matches in Australia over ten weeks. The schedule included three clashes with the national team in Sydney, with others in Brisbane, Newcastle and Adelaide. On the way home, they played against an Auckland selection which opened the door to a New Zealand tour in 1927. There was even an impromptu game against a Hawaiian lineup, won by the Canadians 6–0.

The 1924 Canadian tour of Australia was the great intersection of the two countries' football paths but Con Jones, the obvious candidate to play some kind of role, had no direct part in it. Jones had been told by his doctor to withdraw from the excitement of the sporting world for the sake of his health, but in any case, he was not formally involved in this kind of administration.

Even so, at least three members of the Canadian touring party were linked to Jones. The manager Jim Adam, key forward Dickie Stobbart and veteran full-back Andy McLean.

Jim Adam was an important figure in Canadian soccer in the first half of the 20th century as a player, manager and administrator based in British Columbia. He was part of a committee formed under the leadership of Con Jones to plan the People Shield tournament in Vancouver as early as 1908, while Dickie Stobbart worked with Jones in the development of a plan for a B.C. professional league.

Andy McLean had also been involved in Jones' professional football ventures and rejoined him at the conclusion of the Australian tour as an official of yet another professional competition, the B.C. Inter-City League, commonly known as the Con Jones Loop.

Australian newspapers reported that overtures to Canada about a tour began in January 1923. A convoluted Canadian team-selection process lasting six weeks involved provinces nominating players and having them assessed by committees for their suitability.

The process looked rigorous on paper but ended up with a touring party having the flavour of a political formula. There were six British Columbia players joined by two players each from Manitoba, Ontario, Saskatchewan, Alberta and Quebec.

Inevitably, a three-month long trip meant many players could not afford to leave jobs and family behind to go to Australia. However, Jim Adam maintained that the side was of good quality and a fair reflection of playing standards in Canada.

Although the six-match series with Australia was lost 3-2, Canada won 11 and drew seven of their 26 tour matches. An added match in New Zealand yielded a 1-1 draw against an Auckland XI.

The two international sides were evenly matched, but the Canadian side was hard-hit by injuries. Many players simply played through the pain of knocks sustained in a string of very physical contests with no replacements available.

Prominent football writer A.J. (Alec) Boyd travelled with the Canadian team from Newcastle to Sydney after their 0-0 draw with Australia. In the sports paper *The Referee*, he describes Bill Linning as being 'scarred and resembling the wreck of the Hesperus' while elsewhere in the train carriage Dickie Stobbart was having a stud wound filled with cotton wool and iodine.

Boyd quotes goalkeeper Harry Mosher saying, 'I'm through with football. I'm tired of seeing the ball.' Three days later, Mosher collided with an opponent in Melbourne and broke his leg. Hank Nosworthy replaced him between the sticks for the remaining eight games.

Both sides observed the diplomatic niceties of complimenting each other but the consequences of overly aggressive matches were plain to see. The Canadians waved goodbye to well-wishers from the deck of their ship at Sydney's Darling Harbour with Mosher on crutches and Harry Chapman leaning on a walking stick.

The best players of each team were awarded medals. Dickie Stobbart was a popular choice as best Canadian while goalkeeper Nick Cartwright took the award for Australia.

The games had been reasonably well-attended and the tour just about broke even. Jim Adam said he would back a proposal to invite Australia to send a team to Canada for a return trip in 1926.

That plan did not materialise, but Canada did tour New Zealand in 1927 with Jim Adam again manager and Hank Nosworthy now included as first-choice goalkeeper. Matches between the two countries were broadcast live on New Zealand radio. The star of New Zealand's 1923 tour of Australia, George Campbell, was one of the commentators along with Dudley Wrathall. A film crew from the Government Publicity Office was also assigned to cover the tour.

The final task for the 1924 Canadian party was a match against Corinthians at Con Jones Park in Vancouver the day after they returned. The English side won 2–1.

Canada's next match was a 1–0 victory over the USA in Montreal in June 1925. Half-back Billy Dierden was the only player from the Pacific adventure to retain his position. Nevertheless, the team's achievements are permanently honoured as a team of distinction in the Canadian Soccer Hall of Fame.

Canada's demonstrated interest in Australia and New Zealand as international opponents is another example of a nascent Pacific football culture. The collapse of the Far Eastern Games after their tenth edition in Manila in 1934 killed off its most obvious manifestation.

The growing ease of travel between North America and Europe made trans-Atlantic football contact simpler and a better option for Canada and the USA. Europe was in any case the most obvious historical reference point among immigrants and where the biggest football action was taking place. Asian football had no profile in North America and never received any consideration, while Australasia's unwillingness to build an international profile without a British focus killed a potentially leading role in the region.

South American countries also looked to Europe and played no part in the development of Asia-Pacific football. During the 1920s and 1930s, South American clubs made tours to Europe, and the Combinado del Pacifico – a squad of players from Chile and Peru relying heavily on top sides Colo Colo and Alianza – at least invoked the name of the Pacific in Europe.

The first full international contact between South America and a country from the other side of the Pacific was in 1974 when Uruguay beat Indonesia 3-2 in Jakarta. On that tour, Uruguay played twice against Australia, drawing 0-0 in Melbourne and losing 2-0 in Sydney. Australia went on to draw 0-0 with Chile in Berlin later that year in a World Cup group match.

Australia did not play against Canada again until the home-and-away World Cup play-offs in 1993 won by Australia in a penalty shootout.

In 1980, Canada defeated New Zealand 4-0 in Vancouver in the two countries' first encounter since the 1920s.

CHAPTER 18
The Scandalous Daughter

The life of Con Jones' youngest daughter was far different to that of her siblings. They moved into professional careers and an orthodox relationship with their parents. The girl born as Victoria Louise Bradley was linked to gambling addiction, fraud, deception and other crimes, and ended up serving a prison sentence.

She left institutional care in Australia at the age of 13 and after some time was taken into the Jones family in Vancouver. Her reckless ways continued, and she mostly lived outside the family orbit but retained her father's financial backing.

Con Jones put a high premium on a stable family life as a foundation for the children's progression to the adult world. The four sons enjoyed outdoor sports such as sailing, cycling and golf, and at home occasionally played as a musical quartet under the guidance of their mother Paula.

Victoria's path was much tougher.

The scandal sheet *Truth* described her as the 'Princess of Australian spielers and confidence tricksters' and a person 'whose name will perhaps go down in the criminal records as the greatest yarn-spinner of her time'.

Victoria's older half sister, Minnie Shortel, renamed Amy Jones, had been torn from her mother's embrace by Thomas Shortel, Con's birth name, in dramatic scenes in a Sydney court room. Although custody of the child was awarded to Shortel, she lived under the care of Annie Johnston. Amy Jones trained as a nurse and worked at Vancouver General Hospital and elsewhere. She married in Canada and subsequently moved to Los Angeles where she died in 1980.

Victoria was born in 1894 to Jane Bradley, who died within two days of the birth. Thomas was not identified on the birth certificate, but he was named as the father when the infant was baptised. Victoria Louise Bradley assumed a variety of names and became a notorious figure on the fringes of the law.

Victoria's mother Jane was the sister of Annie Johnston, the carer of Minnie Shortel, aka Amy Jones. Victoria was nine years old when Amy moved to Vancouver. In the years that followed, Victoria was a troubled girl who ended up at Biloela, the Parramatta Girls School that acquired a dark reputation for strict discipline and child abuse.

She was transferred to another facility at Mittagong, southwest of Sydney, on the grounds of her feeble health. She was finally discharged from Parramatta into Annie Johnston's care at the age of 13, being described as 'an uncontrollable child'.

She went to Canada to join the Con Jones clan when she was 20 years old but did not fit into the family framework. Jones eventually financed the young woman's lifestyle in a way which also kept her away from any scandal closer to home.

Jones wanted to keep the domestic peace, protect his daughter and avoid any damage to his reputation in the community at large. Victoria no doubt knew Con's back story, so had some cards to play if ever there was to be bargaining about her own fate.

Under the name Mary Victoria Johnson, she married hotel proprietor Harry William Sawdon in San Francisco in 1923. The marriage did not last long. During her 20s she took to a life on cruise liners paid for by her father. From the 1920s onward, she went on a whirl of voyages shuttling around the Pacific.

These trips took her to Vancouver, San Francisco, Los Angeles, Honolulu, Sydney, Brisbane, Suva and Kobe. Police evidence in later court cases allege that this was where she developed her range of stories aimed at relieving fellow passengers of their money. Shipboard romances could be lucrative.

Detective-Sergeant Corby gave evidence in a 1940 court hearing that Mrs Sawdon had been living by dishonest means for several years. He said she became friendly with different men and obtained money from them 'on the pretence that she was in a certain condition'. On one occasion, she tried to insure a newborn baby to convince an ex-lover, an officer on the liner Sonoma, that he was the father and should pay up. The baby did not exist.

It seems that men did give her money on other occasions to make her go away and to avoid the public embarrassment of admitting they had been duped. Those men declined to help detectives gathering evidence for their false pretences case against Mrs Sawdon.

She reached the headlines in 1929 when seeking 5,000 pounds in compensation from the wealthy Melbourne manufacturer Frederick Dale for an alleged breach of promise to marry her. Mary Sawdon provided evidence that they had lived together as a couple despite Dale still being married. He left Australia to go to England where his wife, described as a drink addict, died.

Upon his return, the relationship resumed. Mrs Sawdon told of trips to the country with Mr Dale and signing in to hotels as husband and wife. She says Mr Dale introduced her to Prime Minister Stanley Bruce. It could be said she was introduced to two prime ministers. At her appeal, Dale was represented by Robert Menzies K.C., who went on to become Australia's longest-serving prime minister.

Under cross-examination, Mrs Sawdon accepted that she had received money from two other men and several women. She said that she had secured $10,000 in damages from a married man she had sued for seduction in California but had not claimed the money. The second man was also married.

Mrs Sawdon was asked whether she knew the American slang term 'gold-digger'. She did. Counsel put it to her that there were two ways a gold-digger got money out of men – by threatening suicide and to talk about a child.

The court dismissed Mrs Sawdon's case citing the absence of any corroborated evidence of a promise to marry. An appeal was also unsuccessful with the judge observing that having a mistress does not mean a man intends to marry the woman.

In 1932 Mary Whitney, as she was now referring to herself after her marriage to Edward A. Whitney, wheedled 30 pounds from the father of boxer Young Stribling while travelling from Honolulu to Sydney. Young Stribling was a highly rated fighter famous for the number of knockout victories he achieved in the ring, although he lost his highest-profile fight against Germany's Max Schmeling for the heavyweight championship of the world.

Young Stribling died from motorbike crash injuries in 1931. His brother and father were travelling to Sydney when they encountered Mary Whitney at sea and later at her flat in Darlinghurst Road in Kings Cross. She never repaid the 30 pounds, nor did she pay for the plentiful wine she ordered to entertain the Striblings.

She may have been living a long time by dishonest means, but she managed to stay beyond the reach of the law's long arm until 1934 when she recorded her first conviction. After extracting substantial sums from well-off men and women, Mary Whitney was undone by procuring 50 pounds in savings from her hairdresser, Emma Booth, a 21-year-old earning a wage of less than two pounds per week.

Mrs Whitney, still referred to as Mrs Sawdon in Australian courts, took the young woman as a companion and servant on a trip to the races in Sydney and a cruise to Tasmania, 'borrowing' the money before Ms Booth started to doubt Sawdon's stories.

Sawdon was found guilty of obtaining money by false pretences and given a 12-month prison sentence. The custodial term was suspended on condition that she stayed within the law and repaid money to Emma Booth and her father. She took the opportunity to swindle enough money elsewhere to pay off the Booths.

Sawdon's castles in the air finally came crashing down in 1940. Her false pretences case heard a stream of evidence of multiple deceptions mostly based on her assertions that she was temporarily impoverished pending the receipt of an inheritance from the estate of her late father.

Requests for relatively modest sums from well-heeled friends were usually honoured until the total amounts started to cause them discomfort. She would explain that banks, lawyers, red tape and confused international communications had delayed the transfer of 63,000 pounds, a hefty legacy. Witness accounts consistently held that Mrs Sawdon claimed this was her share of a 112,000-pound estate left by Con Jones.

Mrs May Salmon revealed that she and her husband had believed Sawdon and provided her with money since 1934. Movie projection businessman Thomas Archibald accepted Sawdon's credentials after being introduced to her by the assistant Canadian Trade Commissioner who said he knew her family in Vancouver.

Victoria's tall tales were sometimes laced with Hollywood star name-dropping. She also claimed to be related to the world's top golfer, Bobby Jones, the four-time winner of the U.S. Open and one of the great personalities in the history of his sport.

Dr Charles Harrison, medical director of the Wahroonga Sanitorium, was also taken in by her stories and gave her money.

Mary Victoria Sawdon was acquitted of theft but convicted on the false pretence charges. Detective Corby told the court that it appeared the accused had married twice. The first was as Mary Victoria Johnson to a man named

Sawdon in 1923, and again in 1932 under the name of Victoria Louise Jones to a man named Whitney.

Corby said that Mrs Sawdon told him that on the occasion of the second marriage, she was under the influence of liquor, and the following day, when she discovered her husband was an old man, she left him. He said a search of her flat found a huge bundle of lottery tickets.

Judge Hill told Sawdon that she was a dangerous woman to be at large and had ignored her previous opportunity to reform given by the court upon her first conviction. He sentenced her to four years imprisonment.

As she was led from the court, she was reported to have shouted, 'I do hope you are all happy now. You are traitors and scoundrels. The sooner I am dead, the better.'

In the late 1940s, Mary Whitney found employment as a nurse in North Queensland. She worked in Proserpine, Bowen, Mareeba and Herberton. The *Cairns Post* reported that Sister Whitney of Los Angeles, California was a member of the Con Jones family of Vancouver.

She was described in the *Bowen Independent* as a popular member of staff who became well- known as the organiser of Christmas parties for young children born or treated at Bowen Hospital. She was said to have paid for these celebrations from her own pocket, although she wrote to people around the world to ask for donations. A tree was erected under her direction on Christmas Eve, laden with toys, and with a Santa Claus present.

The *Bowen Independent* viewed her as the 'good fairy to the younger inmates of the hospital. Like most good fairies she doesn't look for publicity, but we can't help it if unselfishness shines like a beacon in a selfish world.'

Despite the drama and hardships of her early life, she outlived all of Con and Paula's sons but not her sister. She settled in Townsville in her 50s and led a much less-tumultuous life. Her final days saw her return to Sydney where she died in hospital in 1970. She was 76.

CHAPTER 19

The Con Jones Method

Gambling was always at the heart of Con Jones' operations and its throbbing pulse was never louder than at the Brunswick Sports Club in East Vancouver. This business was the focus of a sensational inquiry in the 1930s.

The Brunswick club's activities were on the edge of British Columbia's business laws determining what was a legitimate social club and what was simply a place to gamble. It was one of many such establishments, but details given in public evidence led to it becoming a centre of notoriety. Breathless newspaper descriptions painted a picture of the Brunswick as one of the most profitable gambling dens in North America.

The gambling setup came to be referred to in newspapers as the 'Con Jones Method'.

Gambling ventures from two-up to tote betting and SP bookmaking had underpinned Shortel's operations back in Sydney. In Vancouver, betting resumed in new clubs which were in effect gambling houses hosting well-attended and lucrative card games. Jones made a fortune.

There had long been a broad tolerance of betting in Vancouver. On one level, the lighter touch of law enforcement was due to a wide acceptance of gambling as a vice which did not have victims beyond the gamblers themselves, so it did not need to be a frontline concern for police. On another level, the laissez-faire attitude came directly from police and political corruption.

After his death, the health of the Con Jones businesses slipped into disrepair due to less- competent management of his assets and a new volatility in the local political environment. Claims and denials of corruption were constants during Jones' time in Vancouver. Inquiries with varying levels of credibility tended to uphold the honour of the city administration or police, or to ridicule critics.

In 1936, reforming mayor Gerry McGeer asked city accountant Wilfred Tucker to review the financial records of the Police Commission. The report from low-profile bureaucrat Tucker was dynamite. It found corruption was rife with payments by crime figures to police commonplace.

Tucker's report was never publicly released, but a new commission of inquiry was launched to examine its findings.

Tucker implicated the mayor in wrongdoing and in effect challenged police chief Foster to deny that hundreds of criminals had paid for police protection. He alleged big-time vice barons went scot-free but smaller fry were prosecuted. A *Vancouver Sun* story on the inquiry report said Tucker asserted that 'a Hastings Street gambling club had a weekly take of $12,000 said to make it the largest of its kind in North America'. This venue was the Brunswick Sports Club of Con Jones.

Public hearings of the commission of inquiry heard sensational testimony like an offer of a $500-a-week bribe to a detective, and the operation of a schedule of pre-warned 'raids' designed to minimise damage to criminal enterprises.

A stream of police officers gave testimony which sounded remarkably alike. Their orchestrated accounts were ridiculed. Tucker attended every day of the hearings but declined to give evidence unless the city supplied him with a lawyer. It did not.

To nobody's surprise, the inquiry exonerated the mayor and the police chief from any wrongdoing and asserted that no police pay-offs had been made in the previous two years, the period of the mayor's administration. The mayor stayed in office. Tucker was fired.

The issue of what did or did not constitute a simple gaming house came to the fore after a police raid of the Brunswick Sports Club and the subsequent arrest and conviction of club steward George Bampton on the charge of unlawfully keeping a common gaming house.

The club was in premises rented from Con Jones Limited and operated by the Jones family. The court found its claim to be a club rested on a membership list which was effectively bogus, it had no annual general meetings, and its financial records were less than credible.

Bampton's conviction was overturned on appeal, but it was ultimately confirmed by the British Columbia Supreme Court.

That decision included a description of how the club operated.

'The basement was used for billiards and snooker pool, and it contained tables for chequers, chess, bridge and other card games. There was also a small library with the daily papers and current magazines. The main floor where the members entered the premises had a number of billiard tables and tables where members played rummy. The top floor was provided with a large number of tables where the members played poker and included a lunch counter and cigar stand. Only members were allowed on the premises and the club supported football and baseball teams. The members playing poker paid one half cent, one cent or two cents per hand according on the size of the game, as a table charge. This charge was collected from each player by the steward before each hand was played. When the premises were raided by the police a large number of tables of poker were in play on the top floor.'

The club was open from nine o'clock in the morning until midnight and was one of many named by police commissioner W.J. McFarlane in 1930s inquiries as operating under 'the Con Jones system'. In the Tucker Inquiry hearings, a rough and perhaps conservative calculation was put forward that each gaming table produced $54 per hour.

A club manager was unable to tell the Tucker Inquiry how much was in a day's 'take' and that money from 'pea pool' tables also went into the pot of the club's revenues. The lack of bookkeeping clearly offered ample opportunity to use the proceeds of a cash business without any level of accountability at all.

Shortly before his death, Jones signed off on changes to the structure of Con Jones Limited, the company running his businesses. Three people only held shares: his wife Paula, his brother Sydney, and his eldest son Thomas. It was Thomas who ran the show.

The board changed as the years wore on, but the Con Jones name remained. The Con Jones Limited company was not wound up until the 1970s.

CHAPTER 20
Remembering Con Jones

The Con Jones memorial at Ocean View Burial Park in Burnaby features a huge and intricate stained-glass religious image over a marble base that is inscribed with the names of Con and Paula Jones and their four sons.

The Jones family tomb dominates the back wall of a hall containing scores of memorials to other individuals and families. His eldest daughter Amy was laid to rest in Los Angeles, and his daughter Victoria was buried at Rookwood Cemetery in Sydney.

It should not be a surprise that the most obvious memorial to Con Jones should be one that he created himself. His ego and desire to make an impact on the world drove him to the top in business and sports promotion.

There is no question that he cared little for rules of conduct if they obstructed his path forward. His new life in Vancouver was financed by the straight-out theft of Melbourne Cup betting money. He had businesses in Canada that raked in cash, did not keep proper accounts, avoided taxes and were on the wrong side of gambling laws.

He also achieved so much in his sporting endeavours that he is recognised in Halls of Fame for two sports – lacrosse and soccer. From a starting point in his mid-30s of no experience in association football, he went on to negotiate international deals with people at the very top of the tree.

His efforts hold lessons for Australian eyes. They demonstrate that ideas and proactive participation in international affairs will prevail over passivity. Obsequious obedience to London, or any single authority that does not value one's own interests very highly, is a recipe for failure.

Consciously or otherwise, Con Jones addressed the task of remaking identities for soccer in Vancouver, for professionalism in sport and for Canada in the world game. Like his transition from Tom Shortel to Con Jones, the changes were not without cost. But they all advanced the causes he backed.

Con Jones is a remarkable sporting character. His story, home and away, should be known in both of his countries.

End Notes

1. The Death of Thomas Shortel

The warrants for the arrest of Thomas and Sydney Shortel describe the men as wearing 'sac' suits. The text here uses the correct term 'sack' suits. The warrants were published in the NSW Police Gazette and Weekly Record of Crime.

It is not clear when the alleged theft of money from Peter Herbert took place

The account of the ransacking drama of Shortel's bookmaking premises relies chiefly on a front page story in the Sportsman. Other stories followed in the *Sportsman* and elsewhere with the most vitriolic attacks on Shortel published in *Truth*.

2. 1904 – The Future is Here

The Shortel joke is on the front page of *Truth (April 3, 1904)*.

Jones' Dominion Day entertainments and questions about the allocation of profits are covered in the Saturday Sunset starting on June 15, 1907.

David Forsyth led a Canadian team on a tour of Britain in 1888 comprising 23 fixtures in sixty days. The Canadians won nine and drew five of the matches.

The entourage of the Pilgrims tour is set out in the Sheffield Independent (August 14, 1905).

3. The Shortels

Tom Shortel and Teresa Campbell's marriage plan was rejected by the first church approached because Tom was too young. He lied about his age on the next occasion and was married by a clergyman who himself had been subject to allegations he tried to steal money.

4. The Süssmilchs

C.B.Süssmilch is prominent in coverage of musical events in Sydney from the 1860s onwards reported by the *Sydney Morning Herald and in the German language press including interstate accounts in the Süd Australische Zeitung.*

Activities of various members of the Süssmilch family were reported in news, arts and social pages of the Sydney Morning Herald, Australian Woman's Weekly and the Daily Telegraph stretching into the 1930s. The Brisbane Courier (September 17, 1927) lists the Emma and Emil Süssmilch singing performance on ABC Radio.

The University of Sydney's Australharmony site gives a comprehensive picture of classical singing and music training in Australia in the colonial era including the Süssmilchs.

5. Pacific Soccer League

The Pacific Coast Association Football League was formed at the Driard Hotel Victoria, British Colombia, on July 25, 1908. The formation of the league led to a clash with the British Columbia Amateur Athletic Union and the collapse of the provincial football association. A long dispute over the creation of a new association and its provincial and national legitimacy reached a tentative conclusion in 1920. Tactical dealing by Con Jones' faction ousted his opponents and ensured British Columbia's full entry into the Dominion of Canada Football Association.

The league changed its name to the Pacific Coast Association Football League. The esteemed Canadian soccer historian Colin Jose cited the Callies 3-0 victory over Rovers at Recreation Park, Vancouver on March 25, 1910 as the first professional match played in Canada. His description of these early days is on the Canadian Soccer History website.

Praise for Con Jones and Will Ellis mainly from Sam Goldman was published in the *Spalding's Guide 1909.*

6. George Parker – King of Empire Football

The rumble of doubt about the honourable amateur reputation of the Corinthians increased after the 1903 tour of South Africa. *Sporting Life (January 9, 1904)* observed that *'some Corinthians players returned with fatter purses than they took out.'*

Sheffield F.C. was founded in 1857 and is recognised by FIFA as the world's oldest continuous club. Parker played as a guest.

Parker's early career is well documented in the Polytechnic Magazine which is available online through the University of Westminster website.

Parker was described as the international editor of The Daily Mirror by Wellington's Evening Post (September 30, 1937) he was on a private trip there.

7. The People Shield

Jones and Ellis widely circulated their plan for the Shield to determine the composition of the national team. It was sent to provincial associations and leading newspapers. It was printed in full in the *Winnipeg Free Press (March 3, 1908)*.

The Shield was explicitly rejected as a competition to find the country's best team by the Ontario Football Association stating in 1906 'the present series managed by Mr Parker cannot be considered under their jurisdiction or for the championship of Canada.'

8. Don't Argue – Con Jones in Vancouver

The Saturday Sunset (January 1st, 1908) describes Con Jones as an advanced student of conductor Francesco d'Auria. The Canadian Encyclopaedia records that D'Auria taught at music conservatories in Toronto, Winnipeg and Minneapolis before settling in Vancouver.

Description of the Connaught Drive house by the Vancouver Heritage Foundation in 2008.

9. Con Jones, Lacrosse and More

Criticism of Jones and his place in lacrosse in the *Daily News. (August 10, 1909).*

A report in the *Daily News* on a lacrosse match dispute *(October 7, 1910) refers to Sydney Jones calling for 'fair play, British fair play, Cockney flavour'.* A rare comment on the sound of the Jones brothers speech. Another *Daily News* story *(October 9, 1911) refers to the ever present straw hat of Con Jones,* a comment on his appearance.

Jones comments on lacrosse's *'dead end'* in the *Daily News. (July 15, 1919).*

10. Con Jones the Pirate and his Swashbuckling Mates

The *Montreal Star feature was reproduced in the Greater Vancouver Chinook (February 1, 1913).*

Jack Johnson's accommodation in Vancouver, his fight against McLaglen and many other stories are addressed in Ken Burns' documentary Unforgiveable Blackness: The Rise and Fall of Jack Johnson.

Daily News reports on Bill Howe's activities while staying with Con Jones (August 28, 1909) say he's working on an international rugby competition featuring England, Wales, New Zealand, Australia, New Zealand, South Africa, USA, Canada and France.

11. Will Ellis – Vancouver's New Zealander

A Will Ellis obituary was published in *The Vancouver Sun (17 September, 1934).*

Will Ellis' military service records can be seen through the New Zealand Defence Force website.

12. Global Football

Sir Gilbert Parker comments reported in the *Daily News. (November 4, 1913).*

The boom in international football could only happen through national teams and national football associations. The greater value of national associations meant a deeper discussion about national identity and how it might be expressed through football. The stagnant British focus of this discourse in Empire countries was being superceded by a much more dynamic discussion in the United States, Europe and Latin America. The pre-World War 1 Spalding's Guide provides excellent examples of the American debates.

Words of encouragement for an Empire football association to co-ordinate tours were regularly uttered by English leaders and encouraged by the likes of Tityrus in the Athletic News. South Africa was active in pursuing the idea and received some support from Australia.

13. Australia's North American Tour

Alexander Knox letter relaying an invitation to tour North America was printed in many newspapers, for example, the *Sydney Morning Herald (August 31, 1912).*

The *Referee* refers to Wynton Barker as 'American soccer's Maecenas'. *(September 4, 1912).*

Sydney Mail on exploiters and mercenaries *(May 28, 1913).*

The *Sydney Morning Herald* reports Commonwealth Football Association view that Australia rejects the tour proposal because 'the American A.F.A. is not affiliated with the F.A.' *(April 2, 1913).*

14. Trans-Pacific Australians

Jack Storr description in the Springfield College magazine *Messasoit (1911).*

Spalding's Football Guide (1918-19) notes U.S.soccer leader Thomas Cahill's links to Kwanglim Kwong.

15. Con Jones in Britain

The Sheffield Independent (February 2, 1914) credits Con Jones and Fred Wall as being responsible for the proposal for the visit of English F.A. Cup finalists to visit Canada.

Various newspapers note the Jones post-war tour including the *Daily Mirror, Birmingham Daily Gazette and Yorkshire Evening Post (both February 28, 1920), the Sunderland Daily Echo (January 31, 1920) and the Glasgow Daily Record (March 18, 1920)*.

16. Con Jones Stadium

British Columbia Soccer Association website history pages describing the status of the stadium and its popularity with players and fans.

17. Canada and the South Pacific

A.J. Boyd's accounts of the Canadian tour in *The Referee are the most comprehensive.*

The Canadians were a popular attraction in New Zealand. The fourth and final 'Test' match at Carlaw Park in Auckland attracted a record soccer crowd estimated to number 23,000 fans.

18. The Scandalous Daughter

Mary Victoria Whitney's *Sydney Morning Herald death notice (December 3, 1970)* mentions her residence in Townsville and death in Sydney. Other papers record her relatively sedate life in rural Queensland.

19. The Con Jones Method

The description of the Brunswick Sports Club is in the BC Supreme Court records.

20. Remembering Con Jones

The commemoration of Con Jones' contributions to the development of football can be seen in the British Columbia Soccer Hall of Fame website.

His contributions to lacross can be seen in the Canadian Lacross Hall of Fame website.

Acknowledgements

Roger Barnes from the British Columbia Soccer Hall of Fame has encouraged and helped me to pursue my interest in Con Jones' football endeavours. The Hall of Fame website is itself an excellent source of information on the game's long struggle on the Pacific Coast. Jason Beck, curator of the British Columbia Sports Hall of Fame, has also been most helpful.

The City of Vancouver Archives, the British Columbia Archives, the Museum of Vancouver, the Vancouver Public Library, and the Royal British Columbia Museum have all proven to be very helpful in locating official documentation of the Jones family's life in Vancouver. The office of New South Wales Births, Deaths, and Marriages has been a reliable source for dates and documentation in Sydney.

My knowledge of day-to-day sports activity relies in no small degree on newspaper coverage in sports specialist and general news publications. The National Library of Australia's Trove service is an excellent provider of the digitised Australian publications of yesteryear; the British Newspaper Archive has also been valuable, as has the University of British Columbia's newspaper record.

The University of Westminster provides online digitised copies of *The Triangle*, which offers a useful account of the changing football world at the end of the 19th and beginning of the 20th century. *The Spalding's Official Football Guide* provides a fascinating insight into North American thinking about the football world during Con Jones' active era.

I would like to thank Michelle Brown in Sydney for her research and ideas about the Jones family and its motivations; Rob Brown in Vancouver for giving me information on the Con Jones legend; and Ronald Greene in Victoria for hosting a charming evening of education on Jones' use of tokens in his establishments.

John Fuller, author of *Fame, Fortune, and Fear: The Rise and Fall of Con Jones*, has generously provided photographs for this book.

Even with the assistance of all of those mentioned above, any errors in this book are mine alone.

More really good football books from Fair Play Publishing

Encyclopedia of Matildas Beyond the World Cup 2023

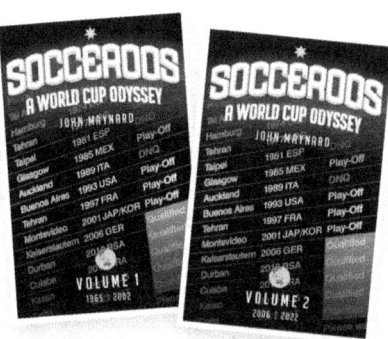

Socceroos – A World Cup Odyssey, 1965 to 2022 Volumes 1 and 2

The Coping Stone

Noddy, The Untold Story of Adrian Alston

Socceroos in Scotland

Playing for Australia

Football Fans In Their Own Write...

Available from
fairplaypublishing.com.au/shop
and all good bookstores

fairplaypublishing.com.au

www.ingramcontent.com/pod-product-compliance
Lightning Source LLC
Chambersburg PA
CBHW052104070526
44584CB00017B/2329